The Fairer Death

Ohio University Press Series
on Law, Society, and Politics in the Midwest

SERIES EDITOR: PAUL FINKELMAN

VICTOR L. STREIB

The Fairer Death

EXECUTING WOMEN IN OHIO

Ohio University Press Athens

Ohio University Press, Athens, Ohio 45701
www.ohio.edu/oupress
© 2006 by Ohio University Press

Printed in the United States of America

Ohio University Press books are printed on acid-free paper ⊗ ™

13 12 11 10 09 08 07 06   5 4 3 2 1

Library of Congress Cataloging-in-Publication Data
Streib, Victor L.
 The fairer death : executing women in Ohio / Victor L. Streib.
   p. cm. — (Ohio University Press series on law, society, and politics in the Midwest)
 Includes bibliographical references and index.
 ISBN-13: 978-0-8214-1693-8 (cloth : alk. paper)
 ISBN-10: 0-8214-1693-6 (cloth : alk. paper)
 ISBN-13: 978-0-8214-1694-5 (pbk. : alk. paper)
 ISBN-10: 0-8214-1694-4 (pbk. : alk. paper)
 1. Capital punishment—Ohio—History—Case studies. 2. Female offenders—Ohio—
History—Case studies. 3. Trials (Murder)—Ohio—History—Cases. I. Title. II. Series.
 HV8699.U5S76 2006
 364.66082'09771—dc22

                                                                        2006011308

To Lynn, and to Noah and Jessi

CONTENTS

PREFACE AND ACKNOWLEDGMENTS

This book tells the stories of fifteen women in Ohio. Included are lots of law and facts about the phenomenon of the death penalty for female offenders, but the focus remains on these unique stories. Study the details of these stories, stare at the photographs of these women, and join me in trying to figure out how each of them came to be damned and condemned by our legal system. Learning these women's stories can provide an understanding of women's crimes and the American death penalty system that no amount of law school or other advanced education can match.

I began the study of female offenders and the death penalty in the early 1980s, collecting stacks of information about every girl or woman executed in what is now the United States since 1632 and about every girl or woman sentenced to death since 1973, the beginning of the modern death penalty system. From that information I generated a series of articles, reports, and papers on this practice and I occasionally represented female offenders on death row as an attorney (see, e.g., *Cooper v. State,* 540 N.E.2d 1216 (Ind. 1989)). Living and working in Ohio, I always wanted to do something focused on the Ohio cases. This is that something, planned as a law review article but grown into this book.

The first part of this study provides a general context for all later discussion of sex and gender bias in the death penalty system, both nationally and in Ohio. This entails gaining background on the law of capital punishment in general (chapter 1) and on facts regarding the death penalty for female offenders nationally (chapter 2). Ohio is subject to the same constitutional constraints as other jurisdictions in the United States, and capital punishment law is fairly tightly circumscribed by federal constitutional law as expounded by the U.S. Supreme Court. In turn, the facts of the Ohio cases appear to be fairly representative of cases in other states.

Part II explores the evolution of Ohio death penalty law, beginning with its legal system as part of the Northwest Territory. The fifteen cases explored in this study occurred over nearly two centuries, during which

Ohio's death penalty underwent a continuous—and continuing—evolution. A case decided a century ago, or even a decade ago, could come out differently today or a year from today. Modern death penalty law marches to the drummer of "evolving standards of decency," and this appears to have been true, even if less expressly so, during earlier eras. An examination of Ohio's developing capital punishment law and of patterns of death sentences and executions yields mixed signals. The data for death sentences and executions, both nationally and in Ohio, indicate a fairly strong predisposition against sentencing female offenders to death, and certainly against actually executing them. However, analysis of death penalty law itself, as laid out over two hundred years of Ohio's history, reveals no obvious exclusion of women or even any recognition of an issue of sex bias. As such, Ohio exemplifies the under-the-radar nature of this phenomenon.

Following these background sections, the book moves on in part III to the stories of the only four women actually executed by Ohio throughout its history, at least as of the date of this writing; all were executed prior to the current death penalty era (1973–2005). This research does not seek to identify women who were sentenced to death in Ohio prior to 1973 but not executed. However, national and Ohio-specific data from the current era suggest a strong likelihood that, if four women were executed during this earlier period, perhaps as many as ten times that number were sentenced to death. Of course, we cannot assume that this unknown number of convicted women shared personal characteristics with the four known to have been executed, or even that they committed similar crimes, and we must avoid such extrapolation. On the face of it, these were extremely rare cases. I hope that careful description and analysis will tell us something about how the four were selected for this rare "honor."

Part IV describes in detail the cases of the eleven women sentenced to death in Ohio in the current death penalty era. None have been executed: nine had their sentences either reversed or commuted, and the last two sentences were imposed in 2003 and 2005. I have relied primarily on court records and other presumably reliable sources. However, information is also taken from concurrent coverage by the local press. I fully understand the problems that can result from assuming that newspaper accounts are reliable, and have therefore made every effort to cross-check and verify information taken from media reports. Nonetheless, the reader is cautioned that the facts reported in these case studies may be tainted by the biases and assumptions of the reporters who provided them.

Given these fifteen isolated cases, one wonders if there are common themes. Of the hundreds, perhaps thousands of capital crimes committed by female offenders in Ohio, why were these women singled out for ultimate punishment? What are the common threads, if any, that link the eleven women sentenced to the four women executed? How can the nine women whose sentences were reversed or commuted be distinguished? Part V and the conclusion contain initial, admittedly halting efforts to provide an answer to these questions.

I have written elsewhere on the distinction between two categories of research and its publication: academic research and advocacy research. The broad goal of academic research is to generate and publish accurate information based upon research results, typically driven by the delight of discovery and regardless of whether the information advances or hinders any particular advocacy position or political agenda. In contrast, the much more focused objective of advocacy research is to bolster the arguments of a given client or political effort, aggressively discounting and even burying research results unhelpful to those arguments.

My analysis of these cases is based upon academic research, not advocacy research. As such, it is intended simply to explore an interesting topic rather than to advocate a specific agenda. In the end, it is the life and death stories of these fifteen women that will linger in the memory and that may stimulate us to look for the stories of other women in similar circumstances.

During the twenty-year gestation period of this study, I have had the joy of being a law professor at Cleveland State University and now at Ohio Northern University. In this role, they actually pay me to do what I love to do, and would do, no matter what. The most fun is working daily with the brightest professors and students, talking with them about fascinating topics such as the subject of this book. So many colleagues have helped me over these years that I will resist the urge to name them.

Four law students, however, must not remain anonymous. Mary McGrath played a major role in beginning and continuing this project with me while at Cleveland State in the mid-1980s. Mary received her J.D. from Cleveland State in 1988. Despite that auspicious beginning, this book project then languished, nearly condemned, certainly ignored, and almost forgotten for over a decade before being rescued by my Ohio Northern students. First was Sharon Biasca, who received her J.D. from Ohio Northern in 1998. Given my tendency to have too many projects going on at the same time, this book then was put on the back shelf for a few more years. To the rescue came Kimberly Kislig and Tammy Watson, two women with extraordinary talents and work ethics. Kimberly received her J.D. in 2003, with Tammy following in 2005, both from Ohio Northern. The final members of our team were Paul Finkelman and Gillian Berchowitz at Ohio University Press, who joined with us to bring these words from an electronic computer file to the published book you are reading. Building upon all of their efforts, we were able to push this work to completion during the fall of 2005.

As the above indicates, I have benefited immensely from the time, space, funding, and encouragement provided to me by Ohio Northern University and in the early stages by Cleveland State University. Always my first love, my family, Lynn, Noah, and Jessi, have tolerated my immersion into this seemingly never-ending project. Far more important than their tolerance is their daily encouragement and support for my work, without which you would not be reading these words.

Ada, Ohio
September 2005

Introduction

PICTURE A condemned murderer being sentenced to death, or eating a last meal, or trudging ever-so-reluctantly into the execution chamber. In your mind's eye, do you see this wretched creature as a woman? Most of us would not, given that over 99 percent of the persons executed in the United States are men.[1] Female offenders, both girls and women, are so seldom found on death row that, once condemned, they may be ignored and forgotten.[2]

Of course, occasional media coverage of high-profile executions temporarily raises awareness of the death penalty for women. A modern case with front-page national coverage was that of Karla Faye Tucker, executed in Texas on February 3, 1998.[3] Tucker caught the attention of the popular media in part because of the grisly nature of her crime (murder by pickax) and in part because she was a pretty, photogenic white woman. An example of an earlier but similarly famous case was that of Ruth Brown Snyder, executed in New York on January 12, 1928.[4] Snyder's execution in New York's electric chair was surreptitiously photographed by a journalist, and that shocking photograph appeared the next morning on the front page of the *New York Daily News,* destined to be reprinted many times.[5] Journalistic descriptions of collected cases also abound, often tending to exploit them with lurid details.[6]

I

There have been riveting films based on this theme. Some are built around real women's cases. The Florida case of Aileen Wuornos, executed on October 9, 2002, spawned several films. The best-known was a semificionalized account entitled *Monster,*[7] released in 2003 and starring Charlize Theron, who received both a Golden Globe and an Oscar. The Wuornos case earlier had been the basis for documentary films based upon her real-life behavior.[8] Nearly half a century ago, the 1958 film *I Want to Live*[9] provided a reasonably accurate portrayal of the case of Barbara Graham, executed in California on June 6, 1955. As with Theron's recognition for her portrayal of Wuornos, actress Susan Hayward also won both a Golden Globe and an Oscar for her portrayal of Graham.[10] Other films have portrayed fictionalized women under sentences of death. *Last Dance,* released in 1996, starred Sharon Stone as a woman sentenced to death and actually executed. Based on a composite of several cases, both real and fictional, Stone portrayed a condemned woman who evolves from being a tough, foul-mouthed killer to a nurturing big sister and would-be lover before being executed.[11]

But what of the rest of the women sentenced to death and, in some cases, actually executed? Who were they, and why were these extremely rare women singled out to receive this ultimate punishment? Why are such women so commonly condemned but ignored by the death penalty system, by scholarly research on crime and the death penalty, and to some degree by the popular media? These questions have been asked by authors who have gone before, as when Kathleen O'Shea remarks, "Few though their numbers may be, they are on death row, and for the most part terribly isolated, invisible, and alone." A recent investigative report labels them the "forgotten population." Apparently, there is a similar tendency to ignore such cases in Britain, as well, where "their cases remain almost totally unknown."[12]

Previous studies of the national landscape around the death penalty for women have identified and analyzed systemic themes and issues.[13] However, by their very nature, these studies have not attempted to dig deeply into the experience of any one jurisdiction.[14] The present study, then, is one entry into exploration of this next level of analysis. Ohio is in many ways a typical, middle-of-the-road death penalty state. It is my hope that reflection on Ohio's experience with the death penalty for women may say something valuable about the death penalty in general, in Ohio and beyond.

PART ONE

A Context of Sex Bias

ONE

Capital Crimes

AMONG THE many deficiencies of the American death penalty system is a systemwide bias based upon the sex of the offender.[1] Even though scholars[2] continue to debate both the causes and the impacts of this bias—indeed its very existence[3]—the discrepancy in outcome between men and women as revealed in our execution statistics has been recognized, at least in passing, even by the U.S. Supreme Court.[4] Joan Howarth, a leading scholar on gender issues, has concluded that "Capital jurisprudence—the law for deciding whether to kill—is also a hidden battleground of gender."[5] The working definitions for the gender concepts of masculine and feminine relied upon in this book also come from Professor Howarth: "Masculinity or maleness is a social construction, to which some women have access and from which some men are excluded. Similarly, both men and women can and do exhibit 'female' qualities of emotionality, intense interrelatedness, and contextual reasoning. But just as countless businessmen can wear pink button-down shirts without eradicating the gender from pink and blue, women who are unemotional, hard-driving, and distant are described as masculine."[6]

The author of this book has pushed these conclusions even further in previous work: "This gendering of capital jurisprudence appears to have infected all who come into contact with the entire death penalty system and to have pushed aside concerns about justice and reduction of violent crime."[7] The following two sections discuss, respectively, sources of sex or gender bias in the selection and definition of death penalty crimes, and in the shaping of these crimes under the law through aggravating and mitigating circumstances.

Capital Crimes

Legislatures designate certain crimes as eligible for the death penalty, constrained almost solely by U.S. Supreme Court rulings limiting capital crime essentially to murder.[8] However, even within the crime of capital murder, certain acts receive quite different treatment. Domestic homicide, the killing of relatives and sexual intimates, appears to be discounted in perceived seriousness and punishability, certainly as compared to homicides by and against strangers.[9] The crimes most commonly committed by those on death row today are felony murders, homicides committed during a dangerous felony such as robbery or rape.[10] This shortcut to death row raises serious jurisprudential questions and has a quite different impact upon male offenders and female offenders. Similarly, the tendency to exclude domestic homicides from capital murder, certainly as compared to stranger homicides and felony murders, also leads to the exclusion of women's homicides as compared to men's homicides.[11] One questionable result of this disparity is the societal judgment that convenience store robbers who kill store clerks should face the death penalty more often than mothers who kill their children.[12]

This brief sketch of the definition-of-crime issue illustrates that men and women typically commit different kinds of homicides. Therefore, the attachment of the death penalty to some kinds of murder and not to others can be expected to produce a disparate impact upon males who kill versus females who kill. Similarly, the tendency of prosecutors to seek the death penalty for some kinds of capital murder more often than for other kinds makes a difference as to men and women being sentenced to death. A similar disparate impact from the sex of the offender can be found in the statutory factors pushing the sentencing jury toward or away from the death penalty.

Aggravating and Mitigating Circumstances in
Death Penalty Statutes

Although modern death penalty statutes typically list a variety of express factors to be considered in aggravation or mitigation,[13] no such express consideration of the offender's sex appears in any death penalty statute in the United States. An apparently increasing number of other countries (primarily former Soviet Bloc nations) do include express provisions in their death penalty statutes either excluding female offenders or giving them special mitigation (such as pregnancy and the responsibilities of motherhood) in imposing death sentences.[14] American death penalty statutes provide no such sweeping provisions (except for pregnancy), but schemes of aggravating and mitigating circumstances can and apparently do have a disparate impact.

Consider some typical aggravating circumstances found in death penalty statutes. One is the commission of a murder for hire, either as the hired killer or as the person who hired the killer to commit the homicide.[15] The Ohio statute is broad and straightforward: "The offense was committed for hire."[16] Women convicted of murder are generally more likely than men to have hired a killer to commit their homicide. However, the killers that women hire are almost always men, as are the killers hired by men. Assuming that the hired killers sentenced to death are almost always men regardless of the sex of the person who hired them, the impact of this aggravating factor may militate somewhat against men. Nonetheless, the use of this aggravating factor against the person hiring the killer probably results in a higher percentage of death sentences for women than of death sentences for men.

Another very common aggravating circumstance is the offender's previous record of violent crimes.[17] If the defendant convicted of the present murder also has a previous criminal record of violent crimes, it is more likely that the defendant will receive the death penalty instead of a prison sentence. Again, women convicted of murder are generally less likely than men to have prior convictions for murder, attempted murder, or other violent crimes.[18] Therefore, this aggravating circumstance will be available in a smaller percentage of women's cases than of men's cases. However justifiable this aggravating circumstance may appear to some, it nonetheless strongly favors female capital defendants over male capital defendants.

A third common aggravating circumstance is a finding that the current homicide was part of a felony murder.[19] Common in felony murder formulations within state death penalty statutes are homicides committed during a rape, kidnapping, or armed robbery. The felony murder formulation avoids the requirement of proving the defendant's criminal intent to commit murder, often the most difficult part of a murder prosecution, thus making successful prosecution more likely. In a typical felony murder case, the prosecutor simply proves the defendant's criminal intent to commit the associated felony (robbery, rape, etc.) and the fact that the defendant caused the victim's death during that felony. This application of the felony murder rule has resulted in capital murder convictions for a very high percentage of men on death row but for a much smaller percentage of women on death row.[20] In addition to all of the other concerns about the appropriateness of using the felony murder shortcut to obtain a capital conviction, this aggravating factor tends to punish men more than women.

A final example is the aggravating circumstance of a homicide particularly planned or premeditated.[21] The federal statute provides a good example: "The defendant committed the offense after substantial planning and premeditation to cause the death of a person or commit an act of terrorism."[22] Judges and juries generally find that women convicted of murder are less likely than men to have premeditated their homicides and more likely than men to have killed while impassioned, angry, or in fear.[23]

Mitigating circumstances make the death penalty less likely to be imposed. Like aggravating circumstances, they go both to the seriousness of the crime and to the characteristics of the defendant. A very common mitigating circumstance is that the offender acted under duress or emotional disturbance at the time of the homicide.[24] California lists as a mitigator "Whether or not the offense was committed while the defendant was under the influence of extreme mental or emotional disturbance."[25] The Ohio statute, too, is a typical example of the duress mitigator: "Whether it is unlikely that the offense would have been committed, but for the fact that the offender was under duress, coercion, or strong provocation."[26] This factor is present to varying degrees in many homicide cases, but finding convincing evidence of it usually is quite difficult. Judges and juries generally are more likely to find duress or emotional disturbance for women offenders than for men offenders in homicide cases.[27] Even casual observance of male and female criminal defendants reveals the greater ability of almost all women to manifest their emotional side, providing the defense attorney with a more effective means of demonstrating this mitigating circumstance.

The list of mitigating factors in many death penalty statutes includes the factor that the offender acted under the substantial domination of another.[28] Again, the California statute is a good example: "Whether or not defendant acted under extreme duress or under the substantial domination of another person."[29] The presumed fact pattern is one in which two or more offenders are involved in the homicide and related criminal activity. When a woman commits a homicide jointly with a man, judges and juries generally are more likely to find that the man was the dominant actor. This occurs with all other variables being the same and only the sex of the offender being different.

Probably the most intriguing and debatable mitigating circumstance is the catch-all provision usually found at the end of the list.[30] For example, the Ohio list of mitigating factors ends with "[a]ny other factors that are relevant to the issue of whether the offender should be sentenced to death."[31] This open invitation provides the defense the opportunity to present evidence as to "any other" mitigating circumstance, so long as the mitigating evidence is relevant and material to the nature and circumstances of the crime or to the character and background of the defendant.[32] Judges and juries generally are more likely to find sympathetic factors in the lives and backgrounds of women than those of men in homicide cases, in part because female defendants may be less reluctant to expose these factors than are male defendants.

This brief sketch of the differential treatment of men and women in the national death penalty system identifies two primary sources of this disparity. The first is probably unintentional and usually benign, in that some factors in death penalty law and procedure may not intend to treat women differently but nonetheless do have a disparate impact. Obvious examples are using the felony murder rule and a past record of violent crime in considering the death sentence, both of which are more likely to put a man on death row than a woman, albeit perhaps for good reason. The second source of differential treatment may be subconscious, but certainly not benign. Examples here are assumptions that women who kill are more likely than men who kill to have been acting under emotional disturbance or under the domination of their cofelons. These mitigating factors provide opportunity for biases in favor of women defendants that are quite difficult to support.

The Death Penalty for Women Nationally

BEFORE TURNING to the Ohio cases of women executed and sentenced to death, it is necessary first to examine the national context of this practice.[1] Women are much less likely than men to commit murder, essentially the only crime that might currently result in a death sentence.[2] In fact, women account for about 10 percent of murder arrests nationally. At least some of these murder arrests occur, however, in jurisdictions which don't have the death penalty.[3] In addition, certainly not all of the murders upon which these arrests are based are capital murders.[4] Although the data on the number of women arrested for murder in each jurisdiction during any one time period are fairly reliable, these are police data and provide only police characterizations of the crimes committed. Lacking are the data to describe the number of these murders which were indeed capital murders, a determination made by prosecuting attorneys and not by the police.[5] Nor are there comprehensive, reliable data on the number of murder cases in which capital charges are filed by prosecutors and, of these, the number plea bargained to lesser charges or actually brought to capital trials.

Coming out the other end of this long, dark tunnel of the early stages of the death penalty process, one can state with confidence that women account for only 2 percent of death sentences imposed at the trial level.[6] This appears to be significant, in that 10 percent of murder arrests were of women but only 2 percent of death sentences for murder were handed down to women. The differential becomes even worse: women account for only 1.4 percent of persons presently on death row and 1.1 percent of persons actually executed in the modern era (1973–present). I have already begun to explore possible structural causes of this differential in chapter 1; my effort here is simply to document the actual number of death sentences and executions of female offenders.

Executions of Female Offenders

Actual execution of female offenders is quite rare: only 568 instances have occurred in the 374 years from 1632 through 2005.[7] These are documented cases of lawful executions and exclude lynchings and similar deaths imposed upon females. Beginning with the earliest American colonial period, these 568 executions of females constitute about 2.8 percent of all American executions.[8] Documenting the older executions of female offenders is quite challenging, but there exists fairly complete documentation of these executions since 1900. From 1900 through 2005, only 0.6 percent (50/8,339) of all executions were of women. Table 2.1 below provides these data by year and by executing jurisdiction.

During the last 106 years, nineteen states and the federal government have executed female offenders. This represents approximately half of the U.S. jurisdictions which had the death penalty during that time period. Those executed ranged in age from seventeen-year-old Virginia Christian in Virginia to fifty-eight-year-old Louise Peete in California. Comparing these post-1900 data with data from previous American eras reveals that the practice of executing women is even rarer now than it was in previous centuries.

The current death penalty era began in 1973, even though it did not result in actual executions of any offenders until 1977.[9] The previous death penalty era was terminated by the Supreme Court's 1972 decision in *Furman v. Georgia,*[10] which in effect struck down all then-existing death penalty statutes. However, both Florida and Utah enacted new death

Table 2.1. Executions of Female Offenders, by Jurisdiction, January 1, 1900, through December 31, 2005

Jurisdiction	Date of Execution	Name	Race	Age at Crime
Alabama	01–24–1930	Gilmore, Selena	Black	[adult]
	09–04–1953	Dennison, Earle	White	54
	10–11–1957	Martin, Rhonda Belle	White	48
	05–10–2002	Block, Linda Lyon	White	45
Arizona	02–21–1930	Dugan, Eva	White	49
Arkansas	05–02–2000	Riggs, Christina Marie	White	26
California	11–21–1941	Spinelli, Eithel Leta Juanita	White	52
	04–11–1947	Peete, Louise	White	58
	06–03–1955	Graham, Barbara	White	32
	08–08–1962	Duncan, Elizabeth Ann	White	58
Delaware	06–07–1935	Carey, May H.	White	52
Federal				
(Missouri)	12–18–1953	Heady, Bonnie Brown	White	41
(New York)	06–19–1953	Rosenberg, Ethel[a]	White	32
Florida	03–30–1998	Buenoano, Judias	White	28
	10–09–2002	Wuornos, Aileen	White	33
Georgia	03–05–1945	Baker, Lena	Black	44
Illinois	01–28–1938	Porter, Marie	White	38
Louisiana	02–01–1929	LeBoeuf, Ada	White	38
	02–08–1935	Moore, Julia (aka Powers; aka Williams)	?	[adult]
	11–28–1942	Henri, Toni Jo (aka Annie)	White	26
Mississippi	01–13–1922	Perdue, Pattie	Black	[adult]
	10–13–1922	Knight, Ann	Black	[adult]
	04–29–1937	Holmes, Mary	Black	32
	05–19–1944	Johnson, Mildred Louise (aka James)	Black	34
New York	03–29–1909	Farmer, Mary	White	29
	01–12–1928	Snyder, Ruth Brown	White	33
	08–09–1934	Antonio, Anna	White	27
	06–27–1935	Coo, Eva	White	40

Table 2.1. *(cont.)*

Jurisdiction	Date of Execution	Name	Race	Age at Crime
New York	07–16–1936	Creighton, Mary Francis	White	36
(cont.)	11–16–1944	Fowler, Helen	Black	37
	03–08–1951	Beck, Martha	White	29
North Carolina	01–01–1943	Phillips, Rosana Lightner	Black	25
	12–29–1944	Williams, Bessie May	Black	19
	11–02–1984	Barfield, Velma	White	52
Ohio	12–07–1938	Hahn, Anna Marie	White	32
	01–15–1954	Dean, Dovie Blanche	White	55
	06–12–1954	Butler, Betty	Black	25
Oklahoma	07–17–1903	Wright, Dora	Black	[adult]
	01–11–2001	Allen, Wanda Jean	Black	29
	05–01–2001	Plantz, Marilyn Kay	White	27
	12–04–2001	Smith, Lois Nadeen	White	41
Pennsylvania	02–23–1931	Schroeder, Irene	White	22
	10–14–1946	Sykes, Corrine	Black	22
South Carolina	01–15–1943	Logue, Sue Stidham	White	43
	01–17–1947	Stinette, Rose Marie	Black	49
Texas	02–03–1998	Tucker, Karla Faye	White	38
	02–24–2000	Beets, Betty Lou	White	46
	09–14–2005	Newton, Francis Elaine	Black	21
Vermont	12–08–1905	Rogers, Mary Mabel	White	21
Virginia	08–16–1912	Christian, Virginia	Black	17

[a] Ethel Rosenberg's capital crime was espionage, the only one of these twentieth- and twenty-first-century executions of female offenders which was imposed for a crime other than murder.

penalty statutes before the end of 1972, and fifteen more states followed suit in 1973.

For simplicity of comparison, this analysis marks the beginning as 1973, allowing for a period of six months following the *Furman* decision for the various jurisdictions to reconsider the death penalty. In 1976, the U.S. Supreme Court ruled that most of these early-1970s death penalty statutes were constitutional.[11]

Actual executions began soon thereafter, the first being that of Gary Mark Gilmore on January 17, 1977, in Utah. Executions of women offenders recommenced in 1984, and the last such execution as of this writing was that of Frances Newton in Texas on September 14, 2005. All executions of female offenders in the current era are listed in table 2.2.

Table 2.2. Executions of Female Offenders, by Date of Execution, during Current Era, January 1, 1973, through December 31, 2005

Date of Execution	Date of Crime	State	Name	Race	Age at Crime	Age at Execution
11–02–1984	02–01–1978	N. Carolina	Barfield, Velma	White	52	58
02–03–1998	06–13–1983	Texas	Tucker, Karla Faye	White	23	38
03–30–1998	09–16–1971	Florida	Buenoano, Judias	White	28	54
02–24–2000	08–06–1983	Texas	Beets, Betty Lou	White	46	62
05–02–2000	11–04–1997	Arkansas	Riggs, Christina Marie	White	26	29
01–11–2001	12–01–1988	Oklahoma	Allen, Wanda Jean	Black	29	41
05–01–2001	08–26–1988	Oklahoma	Plantz, Marilyn Kay	White	27	40
12–04–2001	07–04–1982	Oklahoma	Smith, Lois Nadeen	White	41	61
05–10–2002	10–04–1993	Alabama	Block, Linda Lyon	White	45	54
10–09–2002	1989–1990	Florida	Wuornos, Aileen	White	33	46
09–14–2005	04–07–1987	Texas	Newton, Francis	Black	21	40

Only 11 (1.1 percent) of the 1,004 total executions from 1973 through 2005 have been of female offenders. The proportion has changed recently. Only 1 (0.2 percent) of the 434 executions from 1973 to 1997 was of a female offender, whereas since 1998, 10 (1.8 percent) of the 570 total executions have been of female offenders. This recent (1998–2005) execution pace matches almost exactly that beginning in 1900, so it appears that the 1973–97 lull in executions of female offenders was atypical and that the rate now has returned to its historical norm. Three women were executed in 2001, all in Oklahoma, the most executions nationally of women in any one year since 1953.

Death Sentences Imposed upon Female Offenders in the Current Era

A total of 155 death sentences have been imposed upon female offenders from 1973 through 2005. Table 2.3 provides these data by year. These 155

Table 2.3. Death Sentences Imposed upon Female Offenders, by Year, January 1, 1973, through December 31, 2005

Year	Total Death Sentences	Death Sentences for Females	Portion of Total
1973	42	1	2.4%
1974	149	1	0.7%
1975	298	8	2.3%
1976	233	3	1.3%
1977	137	1	0.7%
1978	185	4	2.1%
1979	151	4	2.6%
1980	173	2	1.1%
1981	224	3	1.3%
1982	265	5	1.8%
1983	252	4	1.6%
1984	285	8	2.8%
1985	266	5	1.8%
1986	300	3	1.0%
1987	289	5	1.7%
1988	290	5	1.7%
1989	259	11	4.2%
1990	252	7	2.7%
1991	267	6	2.2%
1992	287	10	3.5%
1993	289	6	2.0%
1994	315	5	1.6%
1995	318	7	2.2%
1996	320	2	0.6%
1997	276	2	0.7%
1998	300	7	2.3%
1999	279	4	1.4%
2000	231	8	3.5%
2001	163	2	1.3%
2002	159	5	3.2%
2003	144	2	1.4%
2004	125	5	4.0%
2005	96[a]	4	4.2%
Total	7,544[a]	154	2.1%

[a] Estimates.

death sentences for female offenders constitute only 2 percent of all death sentences during this period of thirty-three years. The typical annual death sentencing rate for female offenders during the last decade has been between two and seven sentences. The wide fluctuations in the number of women sentenced to death annually are unexplained by changes in statutes, court rulings, or public opinion.

These 155 death sentences for female offenders since 1973 have been imposed by twenty-five individual states and by the federal government, well over half of the thirty-nine death penalty jurisdictions during this time period. The top five states (California, North Carolina, Florida, Texas, and Ohio) account for almost half of all such sentences since 1973. Virginia, a leading death penalty state for male offenders, has imposed only one death sentence on a female offender since 1973. Virginia last executed a female offender in 1912 (Virginia Christian, also the last juvenile female executed in the entire United States).[12] Table 2.4 lists all jurisdictions that have imposed death sentences on women since 1973.

All but one of the death sentences indicated in table 2.4 were imposed by state trial court judges. Also included is one federal death penalty for a female offender. On June 21, 2005, a federal jury in Iowa recommended a death sentence for Angela Johnson, who had been convicted of murdering three adults and two children.[13] She was formally sentenced to death by the federal judge on December 20, 2005.[14]

Women under Death Sentences as of December 31, 2005

Of the 155 death sentences imposed since 1973, only 49 women in seventeen states remained under sentences of death as of late 2005. Table 2.5 provides data describing the offenders and victims in these cases. Over one-quarter (13/49, or 27 percent) of these 49 female offenders killed their husbands or boyfriends, and almost one-quarter (10/49, or 20 percent) killed their children, grandchildren, or other relatives. Two additional women killed both their husbands and their children. The present ages of these female offenders range from twenty-one to seventy-two, and they have been on death row from less than two weeks to nearly twenty years.

More information about each of these forty-nine cases can be found in the appendix, which provides brief case summaries about each of the women, her crimes, and her death sentence. Also indicated is each jurisdiction's last execution of a female offender. Some of these women are on death row in

Table 2.4. Death Sentences for Female Offenders, Ranked by Jurisdiction, January 1, 1973, through December 31, 2005

Rank	Sentencing Jurisdiction	Race of Offender				Total Females Sentenced
		White	Black	Latin	American Indian	
(1)	California	8	3	6	0	17
	Texas	11	6	0	0	17
(3)	North Carolina	10	4	0	2	16
(4)	Florida	11	3	1	0	15
(5)	Ohio	5	6	0	0	11
(6)	Alabama	6	3	0	0	9
(7)	Oklahoma	7	1	0	0	8
(8)	Illinois	1	4	2	0	7
	Mississippi	5	2	0	0	7
	Pennsylvania	3	4	0	0	7
(11)	Georgia	5	1	0	0	6
(12)	Missouri	4	0	1	0	5
(13)	Indiana	2	2	0	0	4
(14)	Arizona	3	0	0	0	3
	Kentucky	3	0	0	0	3
	Maryland	1	0	0	2	3
	New Jersey	3	0	0	0	3
(18)	Arkansas	2	0	0	0	2
	Idaho	2	0	0	0	2
	Louisiana	1	1	0	0	2
	Nevada	1	1	0	0	2
	Tennessee	2	0	0	0	2
(23)	Delaware	1	0	0	0	1
	Federal (Iowa)	1	0	0	0	1
	South Carolina	1	0	0	0	1
	Virginia	1	0	0	0	1
	Total	**100**	**41**	**10**	**4**	**155**

Table 2.5. Characteristics of Offenders and Victims in Female Death Penalty Cases in Force as of December 31, 2005

Offenders

Age at Crime	Age Currently	Race
Ages 18–19 = 4 (8%)	Ages 18–19 = 0 (0%)	Amer. Indian = 1 (2%)
Ages 20–29 = 18 (37%)	Ages 20–29 = 4 (8%)	Black = 14 (29%)
Ages 30–39 = 17 (35%)	Ages 30–39 = 16 (33%)	Latin = 5 (10%)
Ages 40–49 = 7 (14%)	Ages 40–49 = 20 (41%)	White = 29 (59%)
Ages 50–59 = 3 (6%)	Ages 50–59 = 6 (12%)	Total = 49 (100%)
Ages 60–69 = 0 (0%)	Ages 60–70 = 2 (4%)	
Ages 70–79 = 0 (0%)	Ages 70–79 = 1 (2%)	
Total = 49 (100%)	Total = 49 (100%)	

Victims

Age	Race	Sex
Ages 0–10 = 26 (35%)	Asian = 3 (4%)	Male = 45 (61%)
Ages 11–17 = 4 (5%)	Black = 6 (8%)	Female = 29 (39%)
Ages 18–49 = 31 (42%)	Latin = 18 (24%)	Total = 74 (100%)
Ages 50+ = 13 (18%)	White = 46 (62%)	
Total = 74 (100%)	Total = 74 (100%)	

states which have executed women in the current era, for example, Alabama (2002) and Texas (2005). Others are in states which have not engaged in this practice in some time, for example, California (1962) and Pennsylvania (1946). For yet others of these states, the execution of female offenders is at most a distant memory, for example, Kentucky (1868) and Tennessee (1837). Two states, Idaho and Indiana, currently have women on death row but have never actually executed a female offender in their entire histories.

Ohio is a specific example of a death penalty system having the general characteristics described in this and the previous chapter. Ohio's death penalty system is fairly typical, both now and for the last two centuries, and the pattern of death sentencing and executions of men versus women gives at least the appearance of disparate impact and sex bias. Before a case-by-case study, then, the historical development and current status of Ohio death penalty law warrant consideration.

PART TWO

The Evolution of Ohio's Death Penalty

THREE

Earliest Ohio Death Penalty Statutes

OHIO ALWAYS has been a death penalty jurisdiction, even before Ohio was Ohio.[1] In this regard, Ohio certainly was not unusual: "When this country was founded, . . . the practice of punishing criminals by death, moreover, was widespread and by and large acceptable to society."[2] Similarly, when the U.S. Constitution was originally adopted, its framers accepted the death penalty as constitutional without giving it much direct consideration.[3]

It is not surprising, therefore, to find that Ohio's 1788 prestatehood statutes imposed the death penalty for such crimes as treason and murder, as well as for deaths resulting from arson, burglary, or robbery.[4] The definitions of all five crimes referred to possible offenders either with gender-neutral language[5] or with all-encompassing terms.[6] Given that the modern death penalty is limited to the most egregious forms of murder, consider its predecessor from the 1788 territorial statute: "Murder. If any *person or persons* shall with malice aforethought, kill or slay another person, *he, she, or they* so offending, shall be deemed guilty of murder, and upon conviction thereof shall suffer the pains of death."[7]

It is surprising to find that the language of these territorial statutes authorizing the death penalty expressly anticipated that both men and women might receive such punishment. This use of both gender-neutral and all-encompassing language certainly was not universal, as reference to the contemporary language of the Sixth Amendment to the U.S. Constitution reveals: "In all criminal prosecutions, the accused shall enjoy the right . . . to be confronted with the witnesses against *him,* to have compulsory process for obtaining witnesses in *his* favor, and to have the Assistance of Counsel for *his* defence."[8] Nor was the Sixth Amendment alone in using masculine pronouns. The state extradition provision of Article IV refers to returning the offender upon the demand of the state "from which *he* fled."[9] Similarly, the Fifth Amendment provides "No person shall be . . . compelled in any criminal case to be a witness against *himself.*"[10] These are only samples of the common late-eighteenth-century usage of the masculine pronoun in constitutional and statutory language.

In the year after Ohio achieved statehood, the General Assembly passed its first penal code, including a treason statute authorizing the death penalty for "the person or persons so offending."[11] The new state's murder statute was phrased differently from the previous territorial statute but retained gender-neutral language for offenders: "That if *any person* of sound memory and discretion, shall unlawfully kill any human being and in the public peace, with malice aforethought, either express or implied, and being thereof legally convicted, shall suffer death."[12]

Similarly, the 1804 arson statute continued to authorize the death penalty (if a death occurred) against any "person so offending."[13] In contrast, the 1804 rape statute, perhaps for obvious reasons, authorized the death penalty only for men: "That if *any man* shall carnally know any woman, with force and against her consent, or shall carnally know any woman child, under the age of ten years, with or without her consent, *such person* shall be deemed guilty of a rape and on conviction thereof, shall suffer death."[14]

In 1815, General Assembly changed the language in the rape statute to identify the perpetrator as "any person," but it also removed the possibility of a death sentence.[15] The assembly also removed the death penalty option from the 1815 arson statute.[16] By then, at the beginning of its second decade as a state, Ohio authorized the death penalty only for a defendant convicted of committing treason[17] or murder, now including felony murder but still using gender-neutral and all-encompassing language to describe perpetrators: "That if *any person* shall purposely, of deliberate and premeditated malice, or in the perpetration or attempt to perpetrate any rape, arson, robbery or burglary, kill another, every such *person, his or her* aiders, abettors, counselors and procurers shall be deemed guilty of murder in the first degree, and upon conviction thereof shall suffer death."[18]

As discussed in chapter 1, the authorization of the death penalty for felony murder would have facilitated prosecution of capital crimes, but it would have had considerably less impact on women than on men. The 1815 Ohio statutes also provided the death penalty for assisting or procuring someone to commit capital crimes: "That if *any person* shall aid, assist, abet or procure any other person to commit any one of the offences by this act declared criminal . . . ; or, if the principal offender would, upon conviction, be punished with death, then such aider, assister, abettor or procurer, upon conviction, shall in like manner suffer death."[19] One other 1815 statutory provision appears to be the first statewide attempt to ensure uniform means of execution and to designate where such executions were to take place: "That the mode of inflicting the punishment of death in all cases under this act, shall be by hanging by the neck, until the *person* so to be punished shall be dead; & the sheriff, or the coroner in the case of the death, inability or absence of the sheriff of the proper county, in which the sentence of death shall be pronounced by force of this act, shall be the executioner."[20]

All of the statutes authorizing the death penalty for substantive crimes (excluding the 1804 rape statute[21]) used either gender-neutral or all-encompassing language, and this 1815 statute defining the execution method and location is consistent with those statutes. It also makes clear that condemned women are to be executed in the same manner (hanged) as are condemned men. It appears that public hangings in the county where the crimes were committed had been the practice since statehood in 1803, and presumably earlier.[22] However, Ohio actually hanged only one woman under this statute.[23]

FOUR

The Modern Death Penalty Era in Ohio

OHIO CONTINUED to fine-tune its death penalty statutes, but no changes were made of significance to the death penalty for women. The language and terminology used to refer to the perpetrator or defendant remained gender-neutral or all-encompassing, continuing the theme established by the earliest territorial statutes. In the mid-1880s, the statutes required that all executions be imposed by state-level authorities in the state prison instead of by local sheriffs in the county in which the crime had been committed.

> The mode of inflicting the punishment of death shall be by hanging by the neck until the person is dead; and the warden of the Ohio penitentiary, or in case of his death, inability or absence, a deputy warden, shall be the executioner; and when any person shall be sentenced, by any court of the state having competent jurisdiction, to be hanged by the neck until dead, such punishment shall only be inflicted within the walls of the Ohio penitentiary, at Columbus, Ohio, within an enclosure to be prepared for that

purpose under the direction of the warden of the penitentiary and the board of managers thereof, which enclosure shall be higher than the gallows, and so constructed as to exclude public view.[1]

As of the beginning of the twentieth century, the Ohio death penalty statute for murder gave the trial jury the primary responsibility for choosing life or death for the defendant: "Whoever purposely, and either of deliberate and premeditated malice, or by means of poison, or in perpetrating, or attempting to perpetrate, any rape, arson, robbery, or burglary, kills another, is guilty of murder in the first degree, and shall be punished by death, unless the jury trying the accused recommend mercy, in which case the punishment shall be imprisonment in the penitentiary during life."[2]

Ohio's death penalty laws continued largely unchanged during the first two-thirds of the twentieth century. Three other executions of women in Ohio occurred under these versions of the death penalty: one in 1938 and two more in 1954.[3] Ohio's death penalty statute was destined to undergo the same sea change that all jurisdictions encountered in the 1970s.[4] Ohio has not executed any women since 1954, but it has sentenced ten women to death under these post-1970s death penalty statutes, only one of whom currently remains on death row.[5]

The U.S. Supreme Court's 1972 ruling in *Furman v. Georgia*[6] effectively overturned all death penalty statutes then extant. This was recognized by the Ohio Supreme Court just a few months later in *State v. Leigh*.[7] In 1972, the Ohio General Assembly completely rewrote its death penalty statute,[8] hoping to conform with the murky requirements of *Furman v. Georgia*. This 1972 Ohio statute expressly limited mitigation to only three enumerated circumstances:

(1) The victim of the offense induced or facilitated it.

(2) It is unlikely that the offense would have been committed, but for the fact that the offender was under duress, coercion, or strong provocation.

(3) The offense was primarily the product of the offender's psychosis or mental deficiency, though such condition is insufficient to establish the defense of insanity.

The first mitigating circumstance was unlikely to result in sex bias or disparity in sentencing, but the other two could have had that result. As discussed earlier in chapter 1, offender characteristics such as duress, coercion, and mental deficiency might be applied more readily and often to women than to men.

Four Ohio women were sentenced to death under this 1972 statute. The case of Sandra Lockett, the first of four women sentenced to death under this 1972 statute,[9] became the vehicle for its downfall. In *Lockett v. Ohio,* the U.S. Supreme Court held that this list of mitigating circumstances was too restrictive and that the sentencer must be allowed to consider as a mitigating circumstance "any aspect of a defendant's character or record and any of the circumstances of the offense that the defendant proffers as basis for a sentence less than death."[10]

Continuing Ohio's unbroken determination to be a death penalty jurisdiction, the General Assembly once again reacted to a U.S. Supreme Court holding and passed the current statute in October 1981.[11] Ohio's modern death penalty statute appears to have regressed from those enacted two centuries ago, at least in terms of the premise that women might be sentenced to death. While the basic statute authorizing the death penalty for aggravated murder uses gender-neutral terms for the offender,[12] the statute on determining the aggravating circumstance of a prior homicide conviction does contain strikingly gender-specific language: "[T]he *defendant* may elect to have the panel of three judges, if *he* waives trial by jury, or the trial judge, if *he* is tried by jury, determine the existence of that aggravating circumstance."[13] Despite the express language of this statutory right, one presumes that women defendants would have the same rights as male defendants under these circumstances.

Legislators again fell into the trap of gender-specific language in the current Ohio statute providing a capital defendant with the right to raise the defense of being under the age of eighteen at the time of the offense: "A *person* charged with aggravated murder and one or more specifications of an aggravating circumstance may, at trial, raise the matter of *his* age at the time of the alleged commission of the offense and may present evidence at trial that *he* was not eighteen years of age or older at the time of the alleged commission of the offense."[14] In any other death penalty statute, this male-only language might appear to be simply another example of this unfortunate use of terminology. However, this is the provision allowing offenders under age eighteen to be excluded from the death penalty.[15] Earlier death penalty statutes in Ohio did not preclude these juveniles from the death penalty, and Ohio executed nineteen such young persons between 1880 and 1956. All were male; Ohio has never executed a female offender for a crime committed while under age eighteen.[16] Given this history, Ohio may not have seen the need to provide female juvenile offenders the express right to raise the minimum age issue in death penalty cases. Despite these issues of terminology, Ohio's general felony sentencing statute does prohibit express discrimination: "A court that imposes a sentence upon an offender for a felony shall not base the sentence upon the race, ethnic background, *gender,* or religion of the offender."[17] One hopes that both the trial judge and the trial jury heed that admonition.

With only minor changes, Ohio's 1981 death penalty statute continues in force nearly a quarter of a century later. As explored in chapter 1, several provisions common to all modern death penalty statutes tend to have a different impact for men and women. The current Ohio statute, for example, has an express aggravating circumstance that the offense was "committed for hire," and women are more likely than men to have hired a killer.[18] A more recent addition is the aggravating circumstance that the murder victim was "under thirteen years of age,"[19] again a much more common form of murder for women. Of course, the aggravating circumstance of killing the victim during the commission of one of several listed felonies[20] would be more applicable to men's homicides.

Mitigating circumstances within the current statute may have a similarly sex-specific impact. For example, this statute retains the mitigators of the offender acting "under duress, coercion, or strong provocation" and having a "lack of a significant history of prior criminal convictions and delinquency adjudication."[21] Probably also more helpful to women than to men is the mitigating circumstance of a lower degree of participation in the offense.[22] Nonetheless, seven women have been sentenced to death under some version of this 1981 statute.[23]

Patterns of Death Sentencing and Executions

AS A final context for analyzing the case studies of the death penalty for women throughout Ohio history, it may be helpful to consider the overall pattern of Ohio executions during these two centuries. Fairly detailed and complete information exists for the second of these centuries but not for the first. As set out in chapter 3, Ohio had the death penalty even in its prestatehood days as part of the Northwest Territory and immediately after achieving statehood. Prior to 1885, actual executions under these death penalty statutes were carried out in the local area or county in which the crime occurred. After that date, offenders were executed only by state officers at the state prison.

This change in execution locale provides a significant line for dividing the eras of the Ohio death penalty. Because the executions took place on a county-by-county basis in largely rural, pre-1885 Ohio, accurate and detailed information is very difficult to find and to verify. The leading scholar on the history of executions has set the pre-1885 number of Ohio executions at exactly 118.[1] Another observer of capital punishment history concludes that "the best evidence is that, up to this time [1885], Ohio had executed about 120 people."[2] All calculations here will use the figure 118.

Beginning in 1885, Ohio required that all executions take place in the Ohio Penitentiary in Columbus.[3] Prisoners were hanged there from 1885 to 1897,[4] when Ohio switched to the electric chair.[5] In any event, the names, dates, and other information about Ohio executions since 1885 have been carefully collected and organized.[6] Table 5.1 compares these Ohio executions to the national pattern, beginning with the best estimates available for the pre-1890 period and then including post-1890 data that are verified and documented. The point here is not to establish a definitive list of all executions in Ohio and nationally, but to include a best estimate of those executions as a context for an analysis of executions of women in Ohio and nationally.

Table 5.1. Executions Nationally and in Ohio, by Decade, as of December 31, 2005

Decade	Total National Executions[a]	National Executions of Women[b]	Total Ohio Executions[c]	Ohio Executions of Women[d]
pre-1890s	10,000[e]	509	126[f]	1
1890s	1,215	13	28	0
1900s	1,192	2	25	0
1910s	1,039	0	26	0
1920s	1,169	4	85	0
1930s	1,670	11	82	1
1940s	1,288	9	51	0
1950s	716	8	32	2
1960s	191	1	7	0
1970s	3	0	0	0
1980s	117	1	0	0
1990s	478	2	1	0
2000s	369	8	18	0
Total	19,447	568	481	4

[a] Sources of data for total national executions per decade are William J. Bowers, *Legal Homicide: Death as Punishment in America, 1864–1982* (Boston: Northeastern University, 1984) 54, table 2.3; NAACP Legal Defense and Education Fund, Inc., "Death Row USA" (Summer 2005), 9; and the Death Penalty Information Center (Washington, D.C.), http://www.deathpenaltyinfo.org (accessed February 17, 2006).
[b] Sources of data for national executions of women per decade are Victor L. Streib, "Gendering the Death Penalty: Countering Sex Bias in a Masculine Sanctuary," *Ohio State Law Journal* 63, no. 1 (2002): 472–74; Streib, "Death Penalty for Female Offenders," January 10, 2006, 7 (quarterly Web report), http://www.law.onu.edu/faculty/streib/streib.htm; and the author's unpublished inventory of 567 national executions of female offenders since 1632. See Streib, "Gendering the Death Penalty," 472–74.
[c] Sources of data for total Ohio executions are Bowers, *Legal Homicide,* 479–86; and NAACP, "Death Row USA," 10–28. See generally Death Penalty Information Center, http://www.deathpenaltyinfo.org.
[d] For detailed information concerning these four executions of women in Ohio, see chapters 6–9, infra.
[e] The estimate of ten thousand executions prior to the 1890s is taken from the research of Watt Espy at the Capital Punishment Research Project, Headland, Alabama.
[f] Ibid.

Even a simple analysis of the data in table 5.1 indicates the rarity of executions of women, both nationally and in Ohio. Women offenders comprise 2.9 percent of all executions nationally but only 0.9 percent of executions in Ohio. While both numbers are extremely small, the rate of execution of women as a percentage of all executions is over three times as high nationally as it is for Ohio. However, if only the post-1890 executions are considered, these national and Ohio percentages are very similar. At first glance, this suggests that the pre-1890 data may be skewed, perhaps by the high execution rate of slave women in the South, a practice in which Ohio did not participate.

The other significant observation from these data is Ohio's portion of executions nationally. Prior to 1890, executions in Ohio were only 1.2 percent of all executions nationally. For the next thirty years, Ohio steadily accounted for about 2.3 percent of national executions. This percentage more than tripled for the 1920s, a decade in which Ohio executions were 7.3 percent of all executions nationally. Ohio's portion of all executions then dropped down to an average of about 4.5 percent from 1930 through the 1960s. Since 2000, Ohio executions have represented 4.5 percent of national executions, exactly where they were from 1930 through the 1960s.

The recent changes in the annual rate of actual executions indicate that something is going on. Annual executions nationally reached a peak with ninety-eight executions in 1999 (see table 5.2). This is by far the highest

Table 5.2. Annual Executions Nationally, January 1, 1995, through December 31, 2005

Year	Executions
1995	56
1996	45
1997	74
1998	68
1999	98
2000	85
2001	66
2002	71
2003	65
2004	59
2005	60

number of executions for any year since the reinstatement of the death penalty in the early 1970s. The fifty-nine executions carried out during 2004 constitute less than two-thirds of the total executions for 1999. This is a drop of over one-third in just five years, but it is too soon to tell if this trend will continue. Note that only forty-one total executions have occurred during the first half of 2005, forecasting an annual rate of fifty-five probable executions for all of 2005.

When these total national executions are broken down by state, Ohio ranks high for recent executions (2002 through late 2005). As table 5.3 indicates, Texas is the clear leader among executing states, and Oklahoma is but a distant second. Almost all of the top ten executing states are what one would have predicted: the former Confederate states in the Southeast. Ohio is the surprising exception, ranking fourth in total executions during this most recent time period and well ahead of all but one of the southeastern states.

Table 5.3. Leading States in Executions, as of December 31, 2005

Leading States	Executions 2002 through 2005		Total Executions 1973 through 2005	
	Number	Rank	Number	Rank
Texas	42	(1st)	355	(1st)
Ohio	11	(2nd)	19	(13th)
Oklahoma	10	(3rd)	79	(3rd)
North Carolina	9	(4th)	39	(6th)
South Carolina	7	(5th)	35	(8th)
Alabama	6	(6th)	34	(9th)
Georgia	5	(7th)	39	(6th)
Indiana	5		16	(14th)
Missouri	5		66	(4th)
Virginia	5		94	(2nd)
Florida	3	(11th)	60	(5th)
Arkansas	2	(12th)	27	(11th)
California	2		12	(16th)
Maryland	2		5	(20th)
Nevada	2		11	(17th)
Connecticut	1	(16th)	1	(27th)
All other states	2		112	
Total	106		1,004	

Table 5.4 lists the leading states according to the number of prisoners on death row. Consistent with its rank among states leading in recent executions, Ohio ranks fifth among the leading states in current death row populations.

Combining the data from table 5.3 and table 5.4 reveals even more clearly Ohio's leadership in the death penalty's current era. Except for Texas, the states leading Ohio in executions nonetheless have fewer persons now on death row. If death row populations are seen as the supply pipeline and execution rates are seen as the willingness to carry out the death penalty once the offender is sentenced to death, Ohio, California, and Texas are the three leading death penalty states in the United States. Obviously, these are also three of the most populous states, so their death penalty leadership may be generated at least in part by population as well as by other factors.

Table 5.4. States Leading in Death Row Populations as of October 1, 2005[a]	
Leading States	Death Row Populations
(1) California	648
(2) Texas	413
(3) Florida	385
(4) Pennsylvania	231
(5) Ohio	196
(6) North Carolina	195
(7) Alabama	186
(8) Arizona	126
(9) Tennessee	108
(10) Georgia	107
All other states	788
Total	**3,383**

[a] Source of these data is NAACP Legal Defense and Education Fund, Inc., "Death Row USA" (Fall 2005), 26–27.

PART THREE

Women Executed in Ohio
1803–2005

SIX

Hester Foster

Executed on February 9, 1844

LITTLE IS known about the first woman executed in Ohio. She was reported to be a black adult inmate at the Columbus Penitentiary[1] named Esther, Helen, or Hester Foster.[2] The crime which caused her to be incarcerated is apparently lost to history. In the spring of 1843, while in the penitentiary, Foster murdered a fellow inmate, a white woman, by beating her to death with a fire shovel.[3] Foster was assisted in the commission of the crime by "another colored woman" whose trial was continued until "the next term" and whose fate is unknown.[4] As there is no indication of the sentence of this accomplice, one must assume either that she was not sentenced to execution for her participation in the crime or that she died while awaiting trial.

Foster was sentenced to death on January 9, 1844, and an execution date was set for February 9, 1844.[5] Daniel Morgan, a nineteenth-century chronicler, described this first execution of a woman as "truly the greatest event in the history of Columbus."[6] On the execution date, Foster was hanged at 1:30 P.M.[7] on a gallows erected on Penitentiary Hill[8] beside William Young Graham, also known as William Clark.[9] Graham had murdered a prison guard by "beating him down with an axe."[10] The execution was attended by a crowd of thousands of people "of all sizes and sexes"[11] as well as by several local clergy.[12] The day was reported to be one of "noise, confusion, drunkenness and disorder" in which a well-known citizen paid for attendance with his life when he was pushed over in the crowd and trampled by a horse.[13]

Foster's crime was committed "within a few months"[14] of Graham's and was similar enough for them to be categorized together as having committed "murder behind the walls."[15] This similarity may be why they were hanged together and even why Foster received the same sentence as a male. Furthermore, because of the physical beating with a fire shovel, Foster's criminal act was perceived to be brutal and savage. The public was probably additionally unsympathetic to Foster, a black prisoner, because her victim was white.

SEVEN

Anna Marie Hahn

Executed on December 7, 1938

ANNA MARIE Hahn, the second woman to be executed in Ohio, re-ceived an enormous amount of media coverage as "one of the greatest mass murderers of history."[1] Certainly there was no indication in Hahn's early life that she would die at the age of thirty-two in the electric chair. Hahn was born Anna Marie Filser on July 7, 1906, in Fuessen, Germany.[2] She was the last of twelve children born to respected, devout Catholic parents who were "well-to-do German people that were always thinking about their children and that they should be raised right and get the best they could give them." Her childhood years were "the same as any other normal girl." Reportedly, Hahn had several accidents while bicycling, ice skating, and skiing that led to unconsciousness. Hahn also contracted such illnesses as blood poisoning, goiter, and scarlet fever. She subsequently stated her belief that these accidents and illnesses may have led to "her mind changing that [she] could do the things that happened."[3]

When she was seventeen, Hahn met the man who became the father of her son, Oscar. Hahn said that they fell in love, that he said they would get married some day, and that these were "the happiest days of [her] life." When Hahn became pregnant and told Oscar's father that they would have to get married right away, he told her that he was already married and suggested she abort the child. Hahn reportedly felt "just like a mountain was falling on top of [her], not killing [her] but just smothering [her] and crushing [her]."[4] When Hahn's family learned that she was going to have a baby out of wedlock, Hahn was sent to Holland to live with a sister until her baby was born, but then returned to Germany.[5] At age twenty-two, Hahn left Germany because she "could no longer stand those things that people were saying about [her] misfortune . . . [and she was] afraid that [her son] would understand those things." Also, "these things [that people were saying] were hurting [her] mother who was caring for [her] boy."[6]

Hahn emigrated to the United States, landing in New York on February 12, 1929.[7] The money used to buy her transportation from Germany was supplied by her step-uncle, a seventy-four-year-old retired carpenter, who lived in Cincinnati. Hahn had written him in 1928, telling him that she wished to come to the United States and would repay him if he would lend her money for the trip. She mentioned that she thought she would have little trouble finding work as a housekeeper. Hahn was not in Cincinnati long before her uncle noticed that she was more than able to take care of her own financial needs. Actually, "she did so well in such a short time, and was so secretive about the acquirement of articles too expensive for a housework girl that her uncle elected to avoid her."[8]

Hahn met her husband, Philip Hahn, a telegrapher, at a German dance.[9] He wanted to marry, and she agreed, with the condition that she be allowed to bring her son from Germany to live with them.[10] Approximately three months after their first meeting, the two were married on May 5, 1930, in Buffalo, New York.[11] In July, Mrs. Hahn returned to Germany and brought back Oscar, who was then approximately six years old.[12] Mr. and Mrs. Hahn started their own business, but the business was unsuccessful and "times were bad."[13] The Hahn family moved in with a boyhood friend of Mrs. Hahn's father, who left his house to her when he died. By then, Philip

Hahn was unemployed. Mrs. Hahn started to worry about her son's future as creditors threatened to take away her house. At this time, she started gambling.[14]

Hahn became a familiar figure in handbook establishments. Allegedly, Mrs. Hahn's "penchant for gambling" led to a scheme of "murder for profit" culminating in the death of at least four men and her sentence of death. Hahn was initially arrested in Cincinnati on August 10, 1937, for the Colorado Springs, Colorado, theft of two rings of little value.[15] After her arrest, an investigation of her affairs unfolded one of the strangest stories ever heard in a courtroom.

Hahn regularly visited Dr. Vos, a physician whose office was in a building Hahn owned and occupied. Vos discovered that many of his blank prescription forms were missing. Philip Hahn came forward with a bottle of poison and informed police that his wife had stolen the prescription forms, forged the physician's signature on them, and then ordered the poisons from the local druggist, sending Oscar, who was then twelve years old, to fetch the prescriptions.[16] One druggist reported that Hahn had sent Oscar to get some poison but that he had refused to sell it due to the boy's age.[17] Philip Hahn also claimed that Hahn twice had tried to insure his life for $25,000 but that he had refused.[18] After he refused to be insured, Philip Hahn claimed that he himself became ill with the same symptoms as his wife's victims, and, over Hahn's protests, he was taken to the hospital by his mother. His symptoms were consistent with having been poisoned. Philip Hahn did recover, but the couple soon became permanently estranged.[19]

A search was made of the premises in which Hahn lived. A bottle containing more than seventy grams of arsenic trioxide was found between the rafters in an areaway leading from the first floor to the cellar. At the time the bottle was found, Hahn demanded that it be returned to her and became highly excited and repeated her demand upon a number of occasions, although at trial she denied ownership or knowledge of the bottle. Hahn's pocketbook, which was in her possession at the time of her arrest, was found to be saturated with arsenic.[20]

At first, the police were investigating eleven mysterious deaths.[21] Although a simple autopsy on the embalmed body of one of the dead disclosed no traces of poison, the coroner conducted an exhaustive chemical analysis of the organs from the other corpses.[22] Chemists then determined that sufficient arsenic had been found in the vital organs of four of the dead to cause the deaths of twenty men.[23]

The story of Hahn's murderous spree was laid out by the prosecution in detail. Hahn met George Heis, a coal dealer, in 1936. She borrowed a considerable sum from him to make good on her losses on racehorse bets. Heis began to "dun her for payment of this debt when the coal company from which he purchased his coal pressed him for his bill." Hahn cooked a number of meals for Heis, and he became violently ill and partially paralyzed. The prosecution asserted that Heis's illness had been caused by arsenic, which Hahn administered to him in his food.[24]

Not long after the coal company began to directly press Hahn for payment of the money she owed Heis, she met Albert J. Palmer, a retired railroad watchman who had a modest pension. Hahn borrowed money from Palmer, part of which was used to satisfy the demands of the coal company. Palmer, for whom Hahn had also prepared a number of meals, "became ill, with the same symptoms as those manifested by Heis."[25] Palmer died on March 27, 1937, without diagnosis.[26] The prosecution contended that Palmer had died of arsenic poisoning.[27]

A few months later, Hahn met Jacob Wagner, a seventy-eight-year-old retired gardener, who also had a few thousand dollars.[28] On June 6, 1937,[29] Wagner died in agony, a short time after he had met Hahn and only a day after she had been in his one-room quarters.[30] The next morning, Hahn, knowing of Wagner's death, went to Wagner's bank and presented a check signed by Wagner and made payable to her. When the bank confronted Hahn about the death of Wagner, she admitted she had forged the check. Several days later, Hahn went before the probate court and gained access to Wagner's quarters under the accompaniment of a court deputy. In that room was found a paper purporting to be a will, the terms of which left all of Wagner's property to Hahn. The evidence clearly disclosed that the will was a forgery performed by Hahn.[31] According to the prosecution, Wagner, too, had died of arsenic poisoning.

Not long after Wagner's death, Hahn met George Gsellman, a "pathetic, lonely old man who lived in almost abject poverty."[32] On July 6, 1937,[33] the day after Hahn cooked a meal for the aged Gsellman in his attic room, he died "in agony." The prosecution contended that Gsellman also had died of arsenic poisoning.[34]

Less than a month after the death of Gsellman, Hahn met George Obendorfer, an old German cobbler. Not many days after this meeting, Hahn,

Oscar, and Obendorfer left Cincinnati for Colorado. Obendorfer became violently ill while they were traveling via train near Denver. Hahn took Obendorfer to Colorado Springs, where "he died, forsaken—in a hospital"[35] on August 1, 1937.[36] Obendorfer was buried in a pauper's grave. The prosecution said that he, too, had died of arsenic poisoning administered by Hahn.[37]

Thirty-one-year-old Hahn went on trial for her life just two months and a day after she was arrested.[38] In jury selection, the prosecution asked questions to ascertain whether the prospective jurors might sympathize with Hahn because of her sex. The prosecution also left no doubt that the jury would be asked to send Hahn to the electric chair. Jury selection questions from defense were "directed at establishing whether certain circumstances in . . . [Hahn's] life were of such a nature to prejudice jurors against her, such as her not being a U.S. citizen, having a child out of wedlock, and her penchant for horse-race betting." Hahn's attorney hinted that he might ask for a change of venue on the ground that it was impossible to find jurors who had not formed an opinion on the case because of the widespread publicity.[39] The most frequent reasons offered for excuse from jury service were opposition to capital punishment and unwillingness to consider circumstantial evidence in arriving at a verdict.[40] Ultimately, a jury ranging in age from "twenty-two . . . to several white-haired grandmothers" and composed of eleven women, one man, and a thirteenth alternate male juror was selected. Never before in the history of Hamilton County had the jury in a first-degree murder trial been composed of eleven women and one man. A "murder jury with the feminine element so predominant was extremely rare for all jurisdictions."[41] One wonders if prospective male jurors had expressed sympathy for Hahn's sex and therefore were struck from the jury by the prosecution, but evidence of such bias could not be found.

The state, after first announcing that Hahn would be tried for Gsellman's death, elected instead to try her for the alleged murder of Wagner.[42] The state scored a major victory when the judge ruled, over strenuous objections from the defense, that the prosecutor would be permitted in his opening statement to refer to Hahn's association "with a number of other older men." The state sought to prove that "Wagner's death was only one of a series of planned poison murders through which . . . [Hahn] sought to enrich herself." The defense's "contention [was] that . . . [Hahn] was being tried only for the murder of Wagner and that introduction of any statements tending to link her with the murder of other persons was not admissible." The state's only purpose, the defense attorney declared, was "to inflame and prejudice the minds of the jury." Denying this, the state declared "the purpose was to prove that Wagner's death was only one in a series of murders for profit." In announcing his ruling, the judge said that evidence of motive is always proper for consideration by the jury in a first-degree murder case. The prosecution claimed that personal gain was the common motive in all these acts. Hahn's attorney then asked that the jury be dismissed and that the defense be given more time to prepare its case since "it was not prepared to offer any defense except for the alleged murder of . . . Wagner." The motion was overruled with comment by the judge that both sides had been given six weeks to prepare their cases.[43]

In the prosecution's strong case of circumstantial evidence, physicians and nurses bolstered the contention that Wagner died of a "tremendous dose of arsenic."[44] A toxicologist testified that Wagner had "certainly" died of arsenic poisoning and that arsenic probably was the primary and definitely a contributing factor in the death of Palmer. "Within four feet of the table at which the defendant sat, the poison expert opened large fiber boxes containing virtually all the vital organs of Wagner and Palmer and horror was plainly written for the first time on the face of the German blonde." Consternation, too, was written on the face of her attorney as he declared, "We must sit here open-mouthed because we have never heard of this evidence before." Despite the defense's objection, the physician was permitted to report his findings, and the exhibits were admitted as evidence.[45]

The prosecution's handwriting expert identified Wagner's purported will as a forgery by Hahn. This forgery supplied the monetary motive linking Hahn with the murder of Wagner. The prosecution also won its fight to have admitted as evidence Hahn's white knitted purse, which yielded particles containing 35 percent arsenic. The defense was able to keep from evidence two saltshakers, which the state contended contained 82 percent arsenic trioxide. The prosecution had insisted Obendorfer had died from food well salted from these shakers.[46]

The proceedings were marked by frequent objections from the state and defense.[47] The prosecution sought chiefly to keep the police captain who searched Hahn's house from answering certain questions, while the defense fought to keep Hahn's alleged financial transactions and certain medical testimony from the record.[48] The "eleven women and two men who composed the jury wore a path from the jury box to their room in the rear of the courtroom as the defense attorney fought to keep testimony from the record." Hardly a question was asked to which the defense attorney did not object, and on numerous occasions he insisted upon arguing points with the jury withdrawn. On his second opportunity to cross-examine the police captain, the defense attorney brought out into the open what he had already hinted, when he asked, "Are you sure, Captain Hayes, that you didn't have a bottle of arsenic in your pocket when you searched Mrs. Hahn's house?"[49]

The trial was halted temporarily when the prosecution failed to build a vital link in the evidence. The court adjourned when prosecution admitted it was not able to offer evidence to prove that the embalming matter introduced into Wagner's body at the time of burial had not contained arsenic.[50] Soon thereafter, however, the prosecution supplied evidence that the fluid did not contain arsenic.[51]

During the trial, Hahn was described as a "poker-faced, blonde German woman who at no time displayed any appearance of resentment or shock at anything that has been said." Hahn gazed steadily and unflinchingly at each speaker in turn as they poured forth allegations that could send her to the electric chair. Hahn lost color during the weeks that passed, and deepening lines about her mouth and eyes gave evidence of the strain she had been under, but, outwardly, she was as cool and poised as when first taken into custody. She sat facing the judge's rostrum and at no time turned her head to give even passing notice to the large crowd present. Hahn had the appearance of being entirely alone in her peril and of being resigned to and satisfied with this condition.[52]

After being overruled on his motion for a directed verdict, Hahn's attorney presented a "short and snappy" defense on Hahn's behalf, asserting that the state had "proved nothing."[53] In contrast to the ninety-six witnesses who testified for the prosecution, only three witnesses—Hahn herself, Oscar, and a Chicago toxicologist—appeared for the defense.[54] Oscar testified about the trip he had taken with Obendorfer and his mother and said that he never saw his mother put anything in Obendorfer's food. Oscar also testified about finding a bottle of poison in his home that was not the bottle produced by the prosecution.[55] Hahn followed her son on the stand, and the poison expert immediately followed her.[56] In her story, Hahn "pictured herself as the victim of a cruel coincidence, which found her associated with four men who died unusual deaths." To most of the damaging evidence presented against her by witnesses for the prosecution, "she presented flat denials of fact, insisting that she did not say or do what was imputed to her by these witnesses."[57] From the defense's viewpoint, the "most important aspect of their poison expert's testimony was the declaration that many of the symptoms which the state indicated were present in the victims might have been caused by substances other than poison."[58]

In closing amid the silence of the crowded room, the prosecutor "arose to dramatic heights seldom achieved in a courtroom oratory as he pleaded with the jury to send the blonde defendant to the electric chair." He shouted, "In the four corners of this courtroom are four dead men. These men are pointing their bony fingers at this woman as they say, 'That woman poisoned me. She made me die in agony. She made me suffer the tortures of the damned. Let my death not be in vain.'"[59] The defense attorney followed with a plea that his client be acquitted. He contended that only "vague" circumstantial evidence had been presented against Hahn and that she was a "victim of a cruel sequence of coincidence."[60]

The judge gave Hahn's fate into the hands of the jury at 9:13 P.M. on a Friday night. After deliberating for fifty-two minutes they were sent to their quarters. They resumed their deliberation the next morning at 10:15 A.M. Less than two hours later, at six minutes past noon, the jury arrived at a verdict, finding Hahn guilty and withholding any recommendation for mercy.[61]

The defense immediately filed a motion for a new trial. The grounds for the motion were that irregularities prevented Hahn from receiving a fair trial, that there was misconduct on the part of the prosecution, that there was accident or surprise which ordinary prudence could not prevent, and that there were errors with regard to evidence and of law.[62] Denying the motion, the judge stated that the court was of the opinion that no error had occurred and that "the evidence was so overwhelming that no verdict other than guilty could have been reached by the jury."[63]

Then the judge pronounced the statutory sentence of electrocution, finishing with, "[O]n the 10th day of March, 1938, the said Warden shall cause a current of electricity of sufficient intensity to cause death to pass through the body of the said defendant, the application of such current to be continued until the said defendant is dead, and may God have mercy on your soul." Hahn stood passive before the judge as she heard him sentence her to death. "Only the twitching of her facial muscles showed the strain that she was under." Hahn walked firmly to the elevator; however, while awaiting the elevator, her resolve started to crumble. Tears came freely, and then she ran up to the women's quarters where she collapsed. Her outburst of grief could be heard throughout the quarters. This continued for several minutes until she fainted and the jail physician was called.[64]

In an appeal to the Ohio Court of Appeals for Hamilton County, counsel for Hahn insisted that Hahn was not given a fair trial and that prejudicial error had intervened. In the defense's brief, five specific charges of error were made. Those charges were that a request for a bill of particulars was denied, that there was misconduct by the prosecution, that the judge failed to inform the jury of lesser offenses typically included in first-degree murder charges, that the required degree of proof was not met, and that the admission of evidence regarding the deaths of men other than Wagner constituted prejudicial error. The appeals court affirmed the lower court, ruling that Hahn had a fair trial and that no error intervened to her prejudice.[65] The Ohio Supreme Court denied Hahn's appeal, and the U.S. Supreme Court also refused to consider her case.[66] Defense counsel then failed in an unprecedented effort of applying for a rehearing of her case in the Ohio Supreme Court.[67]

Hahn's last hope to escape the electric chair lay in clemency from Governor Martin Davey. The defense counsel wrote a letter to Governor Davey asking for a clemency hearing.[68] At the hearing, Hahn's attorney and Oscar pleaded for Hahn's life to be spared. Oscar said Hahn had been "as good a mother as there is." Hahn's attorney declared that he was convinced that Hahn was either innocent or insane. He asked Governor Davey if he believed "that a person sane, in her right mind, who gave poison as the state contended, would have brought in doctors . . . who could have discovered the poisoning." He assailed the prosecutor for the use of a state statute which permitted the introduction of evidence concerning three other deaths besides Wagner's. He declared that the prosecutor, who was an elected common pleas judge, had political ambitions which influenced his conduct during the trial. Hahn's attorney also contended that the newspapers, in publicizing the case, impeded the selection of an impartial jury and indirectly put words in the mouths of the witnesses. He shouted, "This case will go down as the greatest farce in history."[69]

Governor Davey admitted that the decision on Hahn's fate was one of the most difficult he had ever been called upon to make.[70] However, he refused to intervene. He said that "although something inside [him] sort of rebelled against the idea of allowing a woman to go to the chair" the crimes committed by Hahn were "so cold-blooded, so deliberately planned and executed," that he had no choice but to permit the decision of the courts to stand. In reference to twelve-year-old Oscar, the governor said he felt sorry for the boy but that "his mother has bequeathed him nothing to be proud of."[71]

On the day of execution, the defense tried one last tactic by filing a petition seeking a writ of habeas corpus with the federal court. The petition declared the writ should be granted because the court which originally tried Hahn did not have jurisdiction since Hahn was not told of the crimes for which she was tried and was "rushed to conviction by an irresistible wave of passion." The petition also claimed that it was impossible for Hahn to secure a fair trial because of the crowded courtroom and corridors and that the jury was inflamed and prejudiced by the prosecution's closing argument. The petition charged that the minds of the jury were made up before they accepted service on the case. The federal court judge took the petition under advisement at 2:30 P.M. and did not hand down his unfavorable ruling until a little more than an hour before the electrocution was to commence at 8:00 P.M[72]

Hahn, described as "a pitiful, whimpering creature," went to the electric chair shortly after 8:00 P.M on December 7, 1938. She entered the death chamber in almost a complete state of collapse and crumpled to the floor a few steps after entering the small, square room housing Ohio's electric chair. Hahn begged beseechingly of the warden, "Don't let them do this to me." As the black mask was being adjusted to her face, the priest began the Lord's Prayer with Hahn repeating after him. The priest had just finished the line "deliver me from evil" and Hahn had replied "deliver us" when the first jolting shock of 1,950 volts of electricity crashed into her body. A lazy, metallic-appearing smoke drifted across the small, white room. The current was turned off at 8:10 P.M. Three and a half minutes later Hahn was pronounced dead. The public had expected her to go to her death with the same stoicism she had manifested throughout her trial, but, in the end, she demonstrated a surprising show of emotion.[73]

In the hour before her execution, Hahn had given four letters to her attorneys, two of which were later published as confessions to her crimes.[74] Strangely enough, Hahn's attorney did not immediately examine the letters on the day of execution but rather said that he did not even know to whom they were addressed, that the letters were in a safe, and that he did not intend to examine them for several days.[75] Later, the letters were said to contain a complete confession of the poison murders for which Hahn went to her death and were offered to newspaper syndicates in New York for a reported asking price of $75,000.[76] Hahn, who until the very hour before her death proclaimed innocence, admitted, in death, that she did do the terrible things in almost exactly the same manner and almost for the same reasons that the prosecutor said she did them.[77] Hahn wrote:

> I do not show my feelings. My troubles in life, starting when I had my baby, had taught me how to control my feelings. . . . I don't know what made me do it. All that I can say is that my troubles were so big that it must have turned my mind. I do not try to excuse myself or my actions. They were not me at all. . . . It all seems like a horrible dream. . . . I wanted to cry out that they were trying the other Anna Hahn and not this one sitting in the courtroom. . . . Maybe it would have been different if I had only told my lawyers the truth. My lawyers fought so hard for me. But that is all over now. . . . I do not fear my end and my last concern is only for my boy. I have written this confession with the full knowledge that death is near and I only ask one favor, and that is that my son should not be judged for the wrongs that his mother may have done.[78]

Without regard to the funds derived from the sale of her confession, Hahn's attorneys assured Oscar's future. He was placed in a good school away from Cincinnati under a new name.[79]

In another strange twist to this case, one cannot help but wonder why Oscar was not considered a suspect. Was it perhaps easier in 1938 to believe an adult German woman was capable of these poison murders rather than an angelic-looking twelve-year-old boy? Oscar testified that he played in the cellar, that he had a chemical and microscope set including several bottles with powders and pills in them taken from the back of doctors' offices, and that he sometimes hid his chemicals in the rafters of the cellar where the arsenic bottle was found. He also testified that he was not sure if the bottle of arsenic found in the cellar was his but that it looked like one of his because he "had a lot of bottles like that." In addition, he was on the train with Obendorfer and admitted to giving him food and water. Oscar was also acquainted with all of the other victims and had eaten several meals with at least two of them.[80] Is it pure speculation to imagine that Hahn may have been innocent, at least of the murder charges? Could Oscar have been the perpetrator as part of a boyish experiment or perhaps because of the jealousy he felt toward the men because of the time they spent with his mother? Philip Hahn had come forward to inform police that his wife had stolen prescription forms from Dr. Vos and used them to order poisons from the local druggist, sending Oscar to fetch the order.[81] Could Oscar have stolen the prescription forms and used them to buy the arsenic on his own?

Hahn was by all accounts a clever woman. Why would such a clever woman leave behind plates of food and pots and pans filled with arsenic in the home of one of the victims? Why would she poison Obendorfer on the train when she expected him to pay for their stay at their final destination?[82] Even with the overwhelming amount of evidence produced by the state, Hahn's attorneys seemed convinced of her innocence and fought for her up to the hour before her execution.[83] Her main attorney's health deteriorated as a result of the trial, and he appeared personally devastated by her execution. Did he perhaps know that Oscar had committed the murders? Was Hahn's confession a way to protect her son? With the written confessions after her execution, was she trying to provide for Oscar monetarily and protect him from future criminal proceedings?

Assuming, though, that Hahn did commit the murders, there were a number of factors working against her. While Hahn's criminal acts lacked immediate brutality, her acts were offensive because of the apparent planning involved, or even what seems to have been an agenda. The multiple victims were elderly men who died agonizing deaths, and Hahn's alleged motive was monetary.[84] Hahn showed no emotion during her trial.[85] She was an unwed mother[86] and a gambler.[87] The jury may have sensed that she was sexually involved with the victims in order further her plans. Finally, the media repeatedly characterized Hahn by her German heritage.[88] Undoubtedly, during this era of Hitler's Germany and looming war, her German heritage automatically made her suspect.

One must wonder, however, if Hahn's motive really was monetary. Could she have perhaps just been fulfilling her desire to punish men for the hurt she felt when Oscar's father told her that he was already married?[89] Because one of her victims, Gsellman, was poor,[90] there seems to have been some other motive besides financial gain.

EIGHT

Dovie Blanche Dean

Executed on January 15, 1954

THE THIRD woman executed in Ohio was Dovie Blanche Dean,[1] who was also referred to as Dovie Myers Dean.[2] Dean's case received little news coverage, although the prosecution claimed it was similar to that of Anna Hahn.[3]

Little is known of Dean's early life, but she apparently had a hard adulthood. Dean married at nineteen and within a short period of time gave birth to six children. In 1937, Dean's husband was sentenced to the West Virginia Penitentiary for seven years for the rape of their oldest daughter, who later died in childbirth. In order to raise her children, Dean accepted any type of employment available.[4]

In 1949, after her youngest child was grown, Dean went to live with her daughter and son-in-law in Clermont County, Ohio, where she met

Hawkins Dean, a prosperous sixty-nine-year-old farmer. In January 1952, after his second wife had died, Mr. Dean asked Dean to be his housekeeper. She and her thirty-year-old son, Carl, moved in with Mr. Dean. On April 11, 1952, Dean obtained a divorce from her first husband. The divorce was paid for by Mr. Dean.[5] In a will filed on April 12, 1952,[6] Mr. Dean named Dean the beneficiary of his estate, which was valued between $10,000 and $27,000,[7] but only as a life tenant.[8] They married on the following day.[9] She was fifty-four years old, and he was sixty-nine.[10]

Less than four months later, in early August of 1952, Mr. Dean fell ill with vomiting spells. His daughter discovered that he was ill and said Dean told her that she had not called a doctor because she thought he was suffering from a virus infection and would soon recover. Mr. Dean's daughter called in a doctor, who advised that Mr. Dean be taken to the hospital. Mr. Dean was admitted to the hospital and remained there a week before he was released.[11] Mr. Dean apparently was suspicious of the cause of his illness and requested that his daughter ask for an autopsy in the event of his death.[12] Mr. Dean once again became ill after his return from the hospital, and he died on August 22, 1952, at his farmhouse.[13] Mr. Dean's daughter requested an autopsy, and excessive amounts of arsenic were found in his stomach and other organs,[14] reportedly enough to kill at least three men.[15]

The authorities worked more than sixteen hours a day for two weeks on Mr. Dean's case. Dean, Carl, and Dean's forty-four-year-old son-in-law, Clyde Bryant, were considered the primary suspects. The authorities did not believe Mr. Dean's estate was a motive because the estate was given to Dean for life regardless of whether they married. The authorities did suspect, however, that the motive could have been a relationship believed to have existed between Dean and Bryant. A bottle of arsenic was found in Bryant's car, but the find was of questionable value because an analysis revealed that the arsenic was not the same kind as that found in Mr. Dean's stomach.[16] Several members of Dean's family were fingerprinted,[17] and Dean, Carl, and Bryant were questioned and given lie detector tests.[18]

On September 12, 1952, three weeks after Mr. Dean's death, Dean confessed to his murder.[19] Dean had been held at the jail for nine days without being charged.[20] On the day before the confession, she had been given three lie detector tests and questioned continually for more than twenty-four hours.[21] Dean first accused Carl, but the sheriff, who believed that Carl was innocent because of the results of the lie detector tests, told her that any woman who could accuse her son of such a crime could easily have done it herself. The sheriff then asked Dean if she wanted to change her story, considering that she and Carl were the only suspects.[22] Finally, Dean said, "If the suspects come down to Carl and me, I'll take the rap."[23] Dean confessed at 4:30 A.M. and dictated and signed a full confession at 6:00 A.M., which Carl signed as a witness.[24]

Dean first claimed that Mr. Dean had taken the arsenic himself, but after persistent interrogations she claimed she administered the arsenic to him in self-defense. She said that Mr. Dean, worried over his impotence, had threatened to kill her and then himself, and that she had given him arsenic in his warm milk on seven different occasions because she feared for her own life.[25] Dean asserted that Mr. Dean's death was the climax of violent quarrels[26] over his lack of performance of "husbandly duties."[27] She said that, after he returned from his weeklong hospital stay without the doctors having discovered the cause of his illness, she felt reasonably sure that she could give him the poison without being detected.[28] After her confession, Dean required medical attention.[29]

On September 15, 1952, Dean was indicted for first-degree murder by a specially called grand jury that deliberated for only thirty minutes.[30] Because Dean could receive the death penalty and because of the seriousness of the charges, the court allowed Dean to select any attorney to represent her, the costs of which were to be paid by the court.[31] Dean pleaded not guilty to the charges.[32] Trial was set for October 20, 1952.[33] However, that original trial date was continued to November 17, 1952, to allow an evaluation of Dean's sanity at the Lima State Hospital, where she was committed "for such time as may be required for this determination, but not to exceed one month."[34] Her attorneys were questioning her competence to stand trial but were not offering a legal insanity defense. They contended she was "not now sane," an assertion which was "based upon their personal observation of her."[35] On November 17, 1952, a sanity hearing was held. The sole witness was the superintendent of the Lima State Hospital, who testified that Dean was sane.[36] The court ruled Dean competent to stand trial. Her attorneys later told the court that although they did not believe Dean had a permanent psychotic condition they did believe there was something abnormal about Dean's behavior.[37] The trial date was continued to December 8, 1952.[38]

Defense attorneys informed the court that their defense would be that Mr. Dean committed suicide, and they also asked the court's permission to employ expert witnesses, presumably to attack the testimony of the Lima State Hospital's superintendent that Dean was sane.[39] The prosecution expected to present Dean's motive in killing Mr. Dean as her disappointment over his alleged sexual impotence. Statements regarding Mr. Dean's impotence had been made in Dean's signed confession.[40]

The prosecutor opened by saying that the murder of Mr. Dean was "the most gruesome crime ever committed in Clermont County." The defense pointed out in its opening statement that Dean was "better off with [Mr.] Dean living" because Mr. Dean would have provided for her beyond what she would have received under his will.[41] As the trial progressed, Dean's "eyes never wavered as the prosecution hurled charges of 'murder' and her cool and aloof manner conveyed the impression that her mind was far from the crowded courtroom where she was on trial for her life."[42]

The defense attorneys accused the investigators of employing threats, tricks, and subterfuge in getting Dean's confession and of using profane language. The investigators told Carl that Dean had accused him of the crime; at the same time, they told Dean that Carl had said that she did it. The investigators admitted that they had used this tactic, but they offered to show written statements in which Dean accused Carl and in which Carl likewise said he thought Dean was guilty. The defense accused the prosecution of withholding these prior statements.[43] Even though the defense challenged the admission of the confession as being made under duress, it was admitted into evidence.[44]

The strong case presented against Dean was predicated on the confession, which informed the investigators that rat poison by the brand name Zip was used. Subsequent examination revealed that the poison in Mr. Dean's body was identical to Zip. The examination also confirmed that the poison had to have been administered shortly before death because arsenic does not cumulate in the body.[45] The testimony also revealed that Dean had explained to officials that Mr. Dean was "jealous of her and that she drew away whenever he touched her." She did not love him, and he was very repulsive to her, the statement continued. Dean had told officials that she "had become a Christian."[46] The prosecution, however, referred to Dean as "a cold, calculating, cunning woman, not a sweet old lady."[47]

Dean's behavior during the trial was damaging to her own cause. She was perfectly at ease on the witness stand and on rare occasions smiled. Her broadest smile occurred when she was asked to resume her answer after she had been interrupted by a sharp exchange between the prosecution and her attorney. "I don't recall the question," she said, obviously enjoying the exchange between the attorneys. Dean was accused of clandestinely winking and smiling at members of the jury, and she caused a ripple of laughter in the courtroom when asked if she drank excessively by answering, "Not since I've been in jail." Dean at all times appeared supremely confident, almost to the point of being bored. Her only slight show of emotion occurred when the prosecutor showed her a picture of her husband's body, taken at the morgue. "I'd rather not look at that, please," she said, turning her head.

During final arguments, defense counsel declared that Dean falsely confessed to the poisoning to protect Carl and that Carl gladly witnessed the confession because it helped clear him and Bryant. To cast further doubt upon Carl and Bryant, the defense attorney asked, "Why didn't these two come and testify in behalf of their mother?" The defense also remarked that these two men had asked Mr. Dean's daughter not to let Dean know of their telling the daughter about Mr. Dean's second illness, so as to make Dean look suspicious. In addition, the defense attorney produced evidence to show that Dean attempted to get a doctor for Mr. Dean before Carl and Bryant went to Mr. Dean's daughter and told her that Dean had not called a doctor.[48]

On December 13, 1952, the jury of seven men and five women deliberated for just forty-five minutes before coming back with a guilty verdict without a recommendation of mercy.[49] On December 15, 1952, defense counsel moved for a new trial.[50] The defense cited eight errors as a basis for this new trial, claiming that there was misconduct by the prosecution; that the court admitted improper evidence, including the confession; that the confession was made under duress; that the court refused to admit proper evidence; and that the court refused to give certain charges requested by defense at the conclusion of its general charge to the jury. The defense also contended that the verdict was not sustained by sufficient evidence and was contrary to law.[51]

On February, 25, 1953, the judge denied the motion for a new trial.[52] In particular reference to Dean's confession, he stated that abuse would have been ground for error, but that there was no evidence of the confession having been taken under any abusive conditions.[53] The judge then proceeded to Dean's sentencing. When informed by the court that she might make any statement she desired, Dean responded quietly, "I'm not guilty, that is all I know to say." The judge then sentenced Dean to death and set the execution for June 5, 1953.[54]

The defense brought a second motion for a new trial based on newly discovered evidence concerning Dean's emotional and physical condition in the jail following her confession. This motion was denied on April 5, 1953.[55]

Defense counsel then appealed her conviction and sentencing to the First District Court of Appeals in Cincinnati.[56] The prosecutor filed a brief in response to this appeal on April 9, 1953, contending that the Dean case resembled closely that of Anna Hahn, and almost half of the contents of his brief were excerpts from the charge of the judge to the jury in that trial.[57] The First District Court of Appeals affirmed her conviction and sentence on or about May 21, 1953. The ruling held that there was no evidence in the record justifying a lesser sentence and that Dean was either guilty of the principal charge or not guilty of any crime, since the prosecution claimed Dean willfully administered the poison with intent to kill. The opinion noted that failure of the trial court to instruct the jury to disregard certain statements in question was misconduct but not "prejudicial error."[58] In reference to the claim that Dean confessed only to protect Carl, the court stated that the record indicated Dean confessed so that Carl would not be unjustly charged with a crime she had committed.[59]

Defense counsel then appealed to the Ohio Supreme Court, which extended Dean's execution date until November 6, 1953, while it considered the matter. The court denied relief on October 7, 1953.[60] A few weeks later, it refused a rehearing on Dean's appeal.[61] On October 29, 1953, the Ohio Pardon and Parole Commission held a clemency hearing.[62] Governor Frank Lausche delayed Dean's execution until January 15, 1954, to study her case.[63] At 11:25 A.M. on that date, Governor Lausche announced that he would not interfere with the execution.[64]

January 15, 1954, was a dark and rainy day. Dean arrived at the penitentiary at 6:58 P.M.[65] She spent her last hour in the death house waiting room reading scripture. The condemned woman drank black coffee, but she did not eat any of the cookies the prison chef had also brought. The chef said that Dean was very pleasant and appeared as relaxed as if she was waiting for a television program. Dean, "always the model prisoner, was as considerate of those who watched her die as she had been of her jailers."[66] The twelve newsmen who attended were searched for cameras.[67] Without the slightest hesitation, reluctance, or resistance, and with absolutely no outward show of emotion of any kind, Dean walked unassisted to the death chair and sat down as submissively as if she was getting in a chair at a beauty parlor. The sober, solemn, almost sad expression with which she entered the death house was as unchanging as if it had been chiseled in marble.[68] She sat calmly in the chair and looked at the floor, lowering her eyes as though she were looking at her shoes. She appeared neat, her hair was set, and she had on a new prison dress. Dean was not wearing her glasses, and she never raised her eyes again while in the chair. A Protestant chaplain, a Catholic priest, and the Methodist minister who baptized Dean were also present.[69] They read from Psalm 23, Isaiah, and the hymns "There's a Wideness in God's Mercy," "Fear Thou Not for I Am with Thee," and "What a Friend We Have in Jesus," Dean's favorite.[70] A leather mask was placed over Dean's eyes, and electrodes were attached to her left leg and the top of her skull. Electrocution began at exactly 8:00 P.M. Dean bent slightly forward, gave a backward jerk, and tightened her arms on the armrests. Even though she was dead, she was still to receive about fifty-eight seconds of 1,950 volts of electricity. Death was pronounced at 8:07 P.M.[71]

An undertaker from West Virginia came for Dean's body.[72] She was buried at a snow-covered cemetery near Charleston, West Virginia, on January 17, 1954.[73] Her funeral and burial arrangements were made by her eighty-three-year-old father, John Smarr, of Dunbar, West Virginia, and her children. Three ministers conducted the service at the Dunbar Mountain Mission with her father, three of her four living children, and over eight hundred other people in attendance.[74]

While Dean's criminal act of poisoning her husband was not itself brutal, the amount of arsenic given to Mr. Dean and the alleged motive for the poisoning may have turned the jury against her. An autopsy revealed that Mr. Dean had enough poison in his system to kill at least three men.[75] Dean allegedly killed him over his impotence.[76] However, given the couple's ages, 54 and 69,[77] Mr. Dean's alleged impotence probably was not the motive or at least not the only motive. Perhaps, as was speculated at the time,[78] Dean was romantically involved with her son-in-law, Bryant, and Bryant backed away from the relationship when Dean actually killed Mr. Dean. Or perhaps Dean was mentally ill.[79] Certainly, the jury would have frowned on Dean's lack of emotion and her cool manner and joking during the trial.[80]

It is not clear that the jury was allowed to hear evidence on Dean's earlier life, but her past hardships with her first husband and the financial support of her children[81] must have gained sympathy from those who knew Dean. That her family was well liked in the community may also explain the large number of guests. The other, darker explanation may be simple morbid curiosity about this rare case.

NINE

Betty Butler

Executed on June 12, 1954

VERY LITTLE is known about Betty Butler, the last woman executed in Ohio.[1] Reportedly, Butler, who was black, was twenty-four years old at the time of the crime and living in Cincinnati.[2] She was a destitute mother of two children: a daughter, Quo Vadis, and a son, Donald.[3] For some reason, she was unable to obtain either public assistance or help from her family. She was, however, befriended by the victim, Evelyn Clark, who "offered first to pay her, then keep her, in exchange for sex."[4] Clark was a thirty-year-old black, married female who worked at a paper bag manufacturer.[5] The women apparently lived together. Butler sometimes agreed to grant "intimacy" to Clark but more often she refused. The women had violent quarrels, and on the day of the killing both had been drinking.[6]

On September 6, 1952, shortly before 5:00 P.M., Butler killed Clark in a fight. Butler and Clark had been fishing from a rowboat with forty-two-year-old Deezie Ivory, an acquaintance. Ivory rowed ashore when Butler and Clark began arguing, and the fight ensued shortly afterward.[7] Near the shore of the lake, Butler first attempted to strangle Clark with a hand-kerchief.[8] Clark was rendered unconscious, but she was still alive.[9] According to police, Butler dragged her unconscious rival a hundred feet, into the lake, and held her head under the water until she drowned.[10] As she dragged Clark toward the lake, Butler reportedly said, "If I can't strangle her, I'll drown her."[11] Park rangers who found the dead woman said she was dry from the waist down, indicating, according to them, that Clark had been grasped by the legs and her head forced under the water.[12] Shortly after Butler dunked Clark headfirst into the water, she was heard to remark, "My work is done."[13] The crime was witnessed by two men fishing from a rowboat seventy-five feet from shore.[14]

Park rangers arrived and halted Ivory and Butler as they began to drive away. While Ivory and Butler watched, the rangers pulled Clark to high ground but failed in their attempt to resuscitate her. Butler admitted to killing Clark and was taken to jail after her arrest. Butler gave a signed statement to the officers, and she was charged with murder that same evening.[15]

Ivory was a material witness at the trial.[16] Butler contended that she was "a sex slave and killed the victim by drowning her to escape her perverted intentions." After being found guilty of first-degree murder, Butler was sentenced to die in the electric chair with an execution date set for August 5, 1953.[17]

The appellate court affirmed Butler's conviction and sentence and changed her execution date to January 15, 1954. The execution was further delayed to April 19, 1954, by an appeal to the Ohio Supreme Court, which refused to review her conviction.[18] A request for clemency to Governor Frank Lausche further moved her execution date to June 12, 1954.[19] At noon on June 12, 1954, after meeting with the Pardon and Paroles Board, Governor Lausche announced, "The sentence was warranted and there is no justification for intervention."[20]

In prison, Butler was described as polite but remote. Butler interested herself in drawing, painting, and religion. She attained some degree of skill in working with charcoal and would send her artwork to her young daughter and son. A Methodist before entering prison, Butler was taking instruction in her last weeks in Catholicism from the penitentiary chaplain.[21]

On June 12, 1954, Butler was brought to the penitentiary at 7:00 P.M. and was executed an hour later. She was twenty-six years old at the time of her execution.[22] Butler was calm and quiet and apparently resigned as she walked into the death chamber.[23] She was dressed plainly in a pink or white and black print dress and black and white oxfords and clutched a rosary. She murmured something, observers said, as she went in, but no one caught the words.[24] She calmly sat in the chair, the straps were applied, and three charges of electricity were sent through her body at one-minute intervals. She died with the same calm, detached air that had characterized her fourteen months of waiting in Marysville Reformatory. Butler was pronounced dead by the prison physician at 8:10 P.M.[25]

Like Foster, Butler acted in a particularly brutal manner by drowning Clark.[26] Her determination was evidenced by her comments that if she could not strangle Clark she would drown her, and that her work was done.[27] These comments illustrate Butler's raw aggression. Additionally, Butler's homosexuality, poverty, and drinking would not have rested well with the jury.[28] On the first point, there is reason to believe that lesbians fare worse than other women when faced with the death penalty.[29]

PART FOUR

Women Sentenced to Death in Ohio
1973-2005

TEN

Sandra Lockett

Sentenced in 1975, Reversed in 1978

SANDRA LOCKETT, the first woman sentenced to death in Ohio in the current era, became acquainted with Al Parker and Nathan Earl Dew while she and a friend, Joanne Baxter, were in New Jersey. Parker and Dew accompanied Lockett, Baxter, and Lockett's brother back to Akron, Lockett's hometown.[1] After Lockett was taken to the local methadone clinic for her heroin substitute, Parker and Dew, along with the Locketts but not Baxter, ended up at the Lockett residence.[2] Parker and Dew needed to return to New Jersey, and Dew suggested that he pawn his ring for the money needed. Lockett overheard Dew's suggestion but felt that the ring was too beautiful to pawn and instead suggested a robbery.[3]

Because none of the four had a firearm, Lockett's brother came up with a plan for robbing a pawnshop. They would ask to see a pistol and then load the pistol and use it to rob the pawnshop. Parker had four cartridges in his possession, so he was elected to be the triggerman.[4] No one planned to kill the pawnshop owner during the course of the robbery. Because the owner of the pawnshop knew and would recognize Lockett, she waited in the car just outside. The robbery proceeded as planned until the pawnbroker grabbed the gun when Parker announced the "stickup." The gun went off, and a fatal shot struck the pawnbroker.[5]

Parker was apprehended and charged with aggravated murder with specifications—an offense punishable by death—and aggravated robbery. Prior to trial, Parker pleaded guilty to the murder charge and agreed to testify against Lockett, Lockett's brother, and Dew. In return, the prosecution dropped the aggravated robbery and specifications to the murder charge against Parker, thereby eliminating the possibility that he could receive the death penalty.[6]

Lockett's brother and Dew were later convicted of aggravated murder with specifications. Lockett's brother was sentenced to death, but Dew received a lesser penalty because it was determined his offense was "primarily a product of mental deficiency," one of the three mitigating circumstances specified in the Ohio death penalty statute.[7]

Two weeks before Lockett's trial, the prosecutor offered to permit her to plead guilty to voluntary manslaughter and aggravated robbery, each of which carried a maximum sentence of twenty-five years in prison. Lockett refused. Just prior to trial, the prosecutor offered to dismiss Lockett's other charges and to permit her to plead guilty to aggravated murder without specifications, an offense carrying a mandatory life penalty. Lockett again rejected the offer.[8]

After Parker testified at Lockett's trial, the prosecutor again offered the plea agreement to Lockett, and she again refused.[9] The state offered corroborating evidence of Parker's testimony in the form of several third-party eyewitnesses to the robbery and immediate aftermath.[10] Lockett called her brother and Dew in her defense, but they both invoked their Fifth Amendment rights and refused to testify. Lockett's counsel had told the court that Lockett wished to testify, but Lockett decided to accept her mother's advice to remain silent despite counsel's warning.[11] The defense did not introduce any evidence to rebut the state's case, and the jury found Lockett guilty as charged.[12]

In accordance with Ohio statute, the trial judge requested a presentence report and psychiatric and psychological reports. The reports described

Lockett as a twenty-one-year-old with low-average to average intelligence and not suffering from a mental deficiency. The reports also described her minor criminal history and her prior heroin use, from which she seemed to be "on the road" to recovery. After considering this information, the trial judge concluded that Lockett's actions did not fit under any of the three mitigating factors allowed under the Ohio death penalty statute. The judge then sentenced Lockett to death.[13]

The Court of Appeals for Summit County affirmed the trial court, and the cause came before the Ohio Supreme Court as a matter of right.[14] The Ohio Supreme Court affirmed, stating that there was no error in the voir dire examination upon the imposition of capital punishment, that the record revealed purposeful intent to kill, and that there were no grounds for juror disqualification due to pretrial publicity.[15] The court also ruled that the prosecutor's statement that the evidence was uncontradicted and unrefuted was not a comment upon Lockett's failure to testify, that Lockett failed to meet her burden of proving her offense was primarily a product of mental deficiency, and that the statute imposing upon Lockett the burden of proving mitigation of punishment was not unconstitutional.[16]

Surprisingly, Lockett found a sympathetic ear in the U.S. Supreme Court. While affirming the lower court in all the other asserted errors, the Court remanded Lockett's case based upon her constitutionality argument. This attacked the constitutionality of the Ohio death penalty statute on the ground that it did not give the sentencing judge a full opportunity to consider mitigating circumstances in capital cases, as required by the Eighth and Fourteenth Amendments.[17] The Court ruled that the Ohio death penalty statute allowed a limited number of mitigating circumstances that could be considered by the sentencer and that this limitation was incompatible with the Eighth and Fourteenth Amendments.[18] It concluded that "the Eighth and Fourteenth Amendments require that the sentencer, in all but the rarest kind of capital case, not to be precluded from considering, *as a mitigating factor,* any aspect of the defendant's character or record and any of the circumstances of the offense that the defendant proffers as a basis for a sentence less than death."[19]

In lifting the death penalty facing Lockett, the Court also reprieved 98 other inmates, including 3 other women on death row, at the time more than one-fifth of the nation's total of 487 facing death.[20] In 1993, at the age of thirty-nine and after having served eighteen years in prison, Lockett was released and ordered to serve five years of probation. While grateful for having her life spared, Lockett said she had trouble coping with the outside world, and probation authorities documented violations that could lead to further incarceration. On March 5, 1997, about four years after her release, Lockett was returned to prison for probation violations.[21]

Lockett's case is the first of the Ohio cases involving death-sentenced women in which the offender did not kill the victim. The victim was shot by Parker, while Lockett waited in the car outside.[22] The killing, however, could be seen as particularly offensive for two reasons. First, Lockett knew the victim and must have contributed to the decision that the victim was satisfactory prey. Second, the victim was killed over a trivial situation—essentially, traveling money and a ring.[23]

During the planning and commission of the crime, Lockett also showed some characteristics that are seen as weaknesses or faults and that are typically criticized. For example, one must wonder why Lockett would risk prosecution for the sake of two men she barely knew.[24] The willingness to take on this risk suggests some sort of dependency, low self-esteem, or absolute lawlessness. Did Lockett have total disregard for life and law? Or was she acting so as to impress Dew and Parker, members of the opposite sex? Also, Lockett transitioned from bringing home two men she barely knew to committing a crime for these two men's benefit.[25] These actions seem to be the product of impulsive behavior.

ELEVEN

Alberta Osborne

Sentenced in 1975, Reversed in 1978

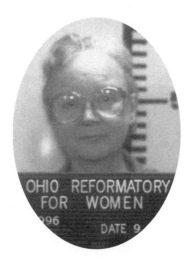

IN 1975, Alberta Osborne became the second woman sentenced to death in Ohio's current era. The victim, the wife of Osborne's lover, was abducted by two men from a grocery store parking lot in Columbus on December 15, 1974, and was later found dead with bullet wounds to the back of her head and neck, ear, and hand and with abrasions and contusions apparently caused by a blunt instrument. Robbery was ruled out as a motive because the victim was still wearing her jewelry and her purse and car were left in the parking lot. During the course of the police investigation, the motive became apparent when officials discovered that Osborne and the victim's husband had been involved in a long-term affair.[1]

On December 30, 1974, Osborne was indicted on counts of kidnapping, aggravated murder, and aggravated murder committed during the course of a kidnapping. Both of the murder charges were with specifications that the murder was for hire and during the course of a kidnapping. The state alleged that Osborne, her son, and her son's friend acted in concert in kidnapping and murdering the victim. Osborne entered a plea of not guilty to all of her charges and was tried separately.[2]

Osborne's counsel filed a pretrial motion asserting that exhaustive news coverage had made it unlikely that a jury could try Osborne free from the influence of that publicity. Her counsel also asserted that the media's influence was aggravated by the fact that the subpoenas served upon prospective jurors contained Osborne's name. The counselor's argument was that a prospective juror, knowing the defendant's name, would avidly read all the coverage on the matter and thereby be biased. The trial court reserved its ruling until after the voir dire examination and then denied the motion.[3]

At trial, Osborne's daughter testified that her mother had told her that she had hired her son and her son's friend to kill the victim for $325 because her lover was leaving her. She also testified that her brother borrowed her car in the early morning hours of December 15, 1974, and that, when he returned it, she was told to use her mother's car to go to work because her brother's friend had become sick in the car and it needed to be cleaned. Osborne's daughter saw her mother go out to the car with a bucket of water, and Osborne had new carpeting installed and all the tires replaced within a few days of the murder. Evidence was presented that pretrial newspaper articles had reported that a tire print was lifted from the scene of the crime.[4]

The victim's husband admitted to a five-year clandestine affair with Osborne. Another witness testified that on the morning of the murder he illegally sold a gun to the friend of Osborne's son and that Osborne's son was present during the transaction. This same witness also testified that he saw the friend of Osborne's son dispose of the gun in a creek. The gun was recovered, and expert testimony, based upon a ballistics report, proved that it was the weapon used during the murder. Two other witnesses, one who had been at the parking lot and one who had been at the scene of the murder, identified Osborne's daughter's car and gave descriptions of the two men who had been in the vehicle. The police testified that bloodstains had been found on the back of the front seat of Osborne's daughter's car and on the shoes of the friend of Osborne's son.[5]

The jury found Osborne guilty of kidnapping and two counts of aggravated murder with the specification that the murder was for hire on both counts. Osborne was not found guilty of the specification that the murder was committed during the course of a kidnapping. A mitigation hearing was held. After hearing the testimony of two psychiatrists, Osborne's brother, employees of the correctional institution, and a missionary who frequented the institution, the trial court found that none of the mitigating circumstances had been established. The court then sentenced Osborne to death.[6]

Osborne appealed to the Court of Appeals for Franklin County, and it affirmed her conviction and sentence.[7] Osborne then appealed to the Ohio Supreme Court as a matter of right.[8] In her appeal to the Ohio Supreme Court, Osborne asserted error in the jury selection process, denial of due process, violation of her right to cross-examine, insufficient proof, improper charge to the jury, failure to elect an offense where at least two apply, and improper verdict. Osborne also asserted that Ohio's death penalty statutes were in violation of the Eighth and Fourteenth Amendments and that other parts of Ohio's code were unconstitutional because the statutes did not require comparison of sentences as to attention on either the defendant's characteristics or circumstances surrounding the act, or review or direct review.[9]

The Ohio Supreme Court ruled in 1976 that Osborne was tried by an unbiased jury, that evidence of the hearsay statements made by her alleged conspirators was properly admitted, that the evidence was sufficient to sustain the convictions and to show that the homicide was committed for hire, and that the Ohio death penalty statutes were constitutional.[10] In particular reference to the death penalty statutes, the court noted that Ohio statutes required the death penalty to be imposed upon all defendants convicted of aggravated murder coupled with at least one of the seven aggravating circumstances, provided that none of the three mitigating factors exist. The court reasoned that all similarly situated defendants were sentenced alike. The court also ruled that Ohio's mitigating circumstances were not unconstitutionally narrow because the statute contained the wording "considering the nature and circumstances of the offense and the history, character and condition of the offender" to use when determining whether one or more of the statutory mitigation circumstances was established by a preponderance of the evidence. The court also noted that it had previously ruled that the mitigating circumstances were not to be construed narrowly and that relevant factors, such as prior criminal record and age of defendant, were to be considered by the sentencing authority. Accordingly, the court affirmed the decision of the court of appeals.[11]

As noted in discussing the case of Sandra Lockett (chapter 10), in 1978 the U.S. Supreme Court struck down the Ohio death penalty statute because it allowed only a limited number of mitigating circumstances to be considered by the sentencer.[12] It concluded that "the Eighth and Fourteenth Amendments require that the sentencer, in all but the rarest kind of capital case, not to be precluded from considering, *as a mitigating factor,* any aspect of the defendant's character or record and any of the circumstances of the offense that the defendant proffers as a basis for a sentence less than death."[13] Based upon the *Lockett* ruling, Osborne's death sentence was vacated and her sentence was changed to life imprisonment.[14]

Like Lockett, Osborne did not directly participate in killing the victim. There are, however, certain factors that make this murder particularly offensive. First, Osborne involved her son in the plot. Second, the victim was the wife of Osborne's lover.[15] Third, Osborne wanted the victim murdered because the victim's husband was ending his affair with Osborne.[16]

Also, somewhat like Lockett, Osborne's actions displayed a certain characteristic that is seen as a weakness and that is typically criticized. Osborne's reaction when the husband indicated that he was ending the affair indicates a certain dependency or lack of emotional strength. These characteristics are readily criticized by those who are outside the particular situation.

TWELVE

Patricia Wernert

Sentenced in 1976, Reversed in 1978

FOR TWO murders,[1] Patricia Wernert became the third woman to receive the death penalty in Ohio in the current era. Wernert did not personally commit the murders for which she was charged nor was she present at
the scene of the crime.[2] Instead, prosecutors claimed that Wernert conspired
in a plan in the execution of which her mother-in-law and grandmother-
in-law were bludgeoned to death by a crowbar-wielding assailant, leaving
Wernert and her husband free to inherit the women's estates.[3] Wernert
and her alleged conspirators were tried separately but simultaneously in
the Lucas County Common Pleas Court.[4]

Wernert was thirty-two years old at the time of her arrest.[5] Her marriage
to David Wernert was tumultuous.[6] Wernert claimed that her husband

suffered from post-traumatic stress syndrome as a result of serving in Vietnam[7] and that he was physically and psychologically abusive in the early years of their marriage.[8] A son was born to the couple on September 16, 1963.[9]

About three years prior to the murders, the couple settled in the home of David Wernert's grandmother, Velma Bush, and mother, Harriet Wernert.[10] At the time of their deaths, Mrs. Bush was ninety-six years old, and Mrs. Wernert was sixty-seven. Mrs. Bush and Mrs. Wernert were well thought of in the community.[11]

At the time of the murders, Ottawa Hills was a well-policed two-square-mile village of some forty-five hundred residents. The murders were the first in Ottawa Hills in at least twenty-five years.[12] However, a recent burglary of a house next door had alarmed Mrs. Wernert, and she no longer felt safe in the neighborhood where she had lived for twenty-three years.[13] Wernert claimed that it was this fear that later set in motion the events leading to the murders.[14]

On the evening of November 19, 1975, the police were dispatched to Mrs. Wernert's residence.[15] David Wernert had telephoned the police to report a continuous busy signal on his mother's line.[16] A policeman found Mrs. Bush's body lying in a pool of blood on the kitchen floor, with a wig, broken glasses, and pieces of a hearing aid nearby.[17] Mrs. Bush had been struck seven times in the head with a crowbar and died within minutes of the blows.[18] Mrs. Wernert was found lying face down near the front door of the home. Blood was splattered on the wall and carpeting.[19] She had died almost instantaneously after being struck repeatedly in the head, but the number of blows could not be determined because her skull was fragmented.[20] Mrs. Wernert's poodle-mix dog was found sitting next to her.[21]

Following a weeklong investigation, Patricia and David Wernert were implicated in the crime after an informant tipped authorities that a stolen sports car could be found at their residence.[22] Officers arrived at their home on November 26, 1975, to execute a search warrant for the automobile.[23] The car, which had been repainted from blue to red, was found in the garage.[24] The couple was advised of their Miranda rights but not placed under arrest. Both voluntarily accompanied authorities to the police station.[25]

At the police station, Wernert was again advised of her Miranda rights prior to questioning. She indicated that she understood her rights and signed a waiver form. She then repeated the waiver and agreed to make a statement about the stolen car. Wernert was booked on an automobile theft charge on November 27, 1975, at approximately 2:00 A.M. and placed in a jail cell. While being taken to the cell, she was asked by a matron if she would like to make a telephone call. She replied, "No, my husband will call the attorney upstairs." David Wernert was being detained on another floor of the jail.[26]

Upon further investigation, police determined that the stolen car had been used in the escape of Mrs. Bush's and Mrs. Wernert's killer.[27] Wernert was removed from the cell and again advised of her Miranda rights by a Detective Stiles, who said that he now wanted to question her regarding the murders of her mother-in-law and grandmother-in-law. Wernert again waived her Miranda rights, and in the ensuing interrogation she said that she did not intend for her in-laws to be killed but that her husband and a friend, Richard Arterberry, had talked of "roughing up" the women during a staged robbery in an attempt to frighten them into moving.[28] Arterberry, age twenty-two, had been living with the Wernerts for at least one week and was also in police custody.[29] After this second interrogation, jail telephone records indicate that Wernert attempted to call her family's attorney but could not find the telephone number.[30]

While walking Wernert through the hall to a prearranged meeting with her husband, Detective Stiles told Wernert that her story was inconsistent with a confession made by David Wernert.[31] He said David Wernert had confessed that both he and his wife participated with Arterberry in planning the murders as part of a mercy killing. Detective Stiles and Wernert disagree as to what happened next. Detective Stiles testified at trial that Wernert subsequently admitted to him that her husband's statement was true and that she had lied earlier. However, Wernert took the stand in her defense and denied having told the detective that her husband's confession was truthful.[32] Wernert, David Wernert, and Arterberry each made a tape-recorded statement about the killings while in custody. All three were charged with the murders that afternoon.[33]

Talk of the death penalty for Wernert began just days after her arrest. A December 4, 1975, headline read, "Three Are Indicted in Slaying of Two at Ottawa Hills; Specifications Included Which Could Mean Use of Death Penalty." The article reported that, following a three-hour session, the Lucas County grand jury indicted Wernert for two counts of aggravated murder with prior calculation and design and two counts of aggravated murder in the commission of a felony. Specifications of aggravating circumstances, which under Ohio law allowed for imposition of the death penalty, were attached to each count. Three specifications were attached to the counts alleging aggravated murder by prior calculation and design. These specifications were that the murders were done for hire, that the murders were committed during a burglary, and that the plan was to kill more than one person. Two specifications were attached to the counts alleging aggravated murder in the commission of a felony. These specifications were that the murders were done for hire and that the plan was to kill more than one person.[34]

The victims' wills were soon filed in the Lucas County Probate Court. Mrs. Bush left David and Patricia Wernert $10,000 and the home in which they were living.[35] Mrs. Wernert divided her $240,000 estate between her sons.[36] David Wernert was named as the executor. The victims' attorney was advised by the probate court that under Ohio law a person convicted of aggravated murder cannot inherit from his or her victim, and directed him to seek appointment of a substitute administrator for the two estates.[37]

On December 30, 1975, attorney Peter Wagner, representing both Patricia and David Wernert, appeared before Lucas County Common Pleas Court Judge John Connors Jr. and asked him to consider several motions. Wagner asked for a change of venue, claiming that pretrial publicity had "resulted in sensationalism, speculation, and hostile community sentiment to a degree sufficient to prevent the defendants from receiving a fair and impartial trial." Wagner also requested that the defendants be permitted to undergo psychiatric examinations to determine their sanity and competency to stand trial. Additionally, Wagner asked that each charge against the couple be tried separately and that their bond be reduced. Judge Connors scheduled a hearing on the change of venue motion and granted the request for psychiatric examinations. He denied the request for separate trials on the charges and the request for a bond reduction.[38] Wernert, David Wernert, and Arterberry continued to be held in the county jail, each under a $500,000 bond.[39]

Approximately two months into the pretrial proceedings, attorney Wagner told Wernert that it was a conflict of interest for him to represent both of the Wernerts. He then asked the court to remove him as her counsel.[40]

Attorney Al Wysocki was appointed by the court to represent Patricia Wernert.[41]

On September 13, 1976, after reviewing news coverage of the murders and arrests, Judge Connors denied the Wernerts' request for a change of venue. In doing so, the judge noted that the true test of whether an impartial jury could be found in Lucas County would come at the time of the trials. Judge Connors also ruled that the tape-recorded statements made by the codefendants at the time of their arrest could be admitted as evidence at trial.[42] Wernert had argued that she was unable to intelligently and voluntarily waive her rights at the time of the statements due to the ingestion of drugs and alcohol, lack of sleep and sustenance, and concern for the safety of her son.[43] She also claimed that the tapes had been subsequently altered.[44]

The trials were to be held simultaneously in separate courtrooms,[45] prompting Arterberry to later call the proceedings a "three-ring circus" which resulted in "an insult to justice."[46] Lucas County Prosecutor Anthony Pizza, heading a team of six prosecutors handling the three cases, noted that it was unusual to hold separate trials of several codefendants at the same time. Judges Connors, Robert Franklin Jr., and George Glasser presided over the three trials and decided that such a move was necessary to assure that the verdict in one case did not affect the outcome of another.[47]

Jury selection for all three defendants began on September 13, 1976, following Judge Connors's ruling on the change of venue motion. Jurors were instructed by the judge to ignore news accounts of the trials but were told they would not be sequestered until they began their deliberations. Special security measures were put into effect to control the large number of anticipated spectators at the trials.[48]

Assistant Prosecutor James Bates said in his opening statement that he would present witnesses to testify that Wernert told acquaintances she would pay someone to kill the two women so that she could get control of their estates. In his opening statement, defense attorney Wysocki contended that no physical evidence tied Wernert to the killings and that her tape-recorded statement to police was coerced by Detective Stiles while she was under the influence of alcohol and tranquilizers. He added that Wernert believed that statements made in her home about killing the women were meant as a joke.[49]

On the third day of Wernert's trial, prosecutors played the tape-recorded statement she had made to Detective Stiles. Jurors heard Wernert say that talk about breaking into the victims' home began as a joke but that the Wernerts later decided to carry out the plan.[50] She added that the break-in was planned to scare the women into moving from their home, which was too large for them to manage.[51] She said that Arterberry agreed to commit the break-in but that he was instructed not to hurt Mrs. Bush. Wernert also said she told Arterberry that she did not get along with Mrs. Wernert and would not mind seeing her injured during the incident.[52] However, she contended that, according to the plan, Arterberry was not supposed to murder the women. "Things weren't supposed to go this way," she said. "He was only supposed to shake them up."[53] Wernert added that she did not learn that the two women had been killed until the day after the murders.[54]

Detective Stiles remained on the witness stand for more than five hours. Wysocki questioned him about discrepancies between the times stated at the beginning and ending of the tape and the actual running time of the statement. The detective denied that the tape was stopped at any time.[55] An electronics engineer subsequently testified that he found a one-second erasure on the tape made after the original recording, which was probably caused by equipment used during transcription.[56]

On the fourth day of the trial, Wernert took the stand in her defense. She told the jurors that David Wernert and Arterberry had joked about a break-in to scare the women but that she did not take their discussions seriously. Wernert denied taking part in the planning of the murders and disavowed any knowledge of the existence of such a plan. She stated that she had instructed her husband to call the police on November 19, 1975, after Arterberry told her that he had killed the women. She claimed to have been caught in a terrible dilemma, knowing that Arterberry had killed the women but being afraid to tell authorities because he had threatened her and her son.[57]

The defense rested on day five of the trial after calling a biochemist who testified that Wernert would have still been affected by drugs she took just prior to her arrest when she made the tape-recorded statement to authorities the following morning. In rebuttal, Bates called an expert who testified that the amount of tranquilizing drugs and alcohol that Wernert claimed to have consumed prior to her arrest would have caused her death.[58]

Testimony was also concluding in the trials of Wernert's codefendants. Jurors in Arterberry's trial heard him tell authorities on tape that he "got caught up" in the Wernerts' plan to kill the women after becoming their friend through a mutual interest in auto racing. He said that he believed killing the victims would be a favor to the victims because of their infirmities, which were often referred to by the Wernerts. He added that the couple had told him that Wernert had lung cancer and that "it would be nice" if she could enjoy some of the inheritance money before she died. Arterberry also said on tape that he was never promised money for his actions but that he and David Wernert had discussed entering into business together.[59]

According to Arterberry's taped statement, he and David Wernert visited the victims' home the day of the murders under the pretext of removing some tires stored there. Arterberry concealed himself in the basement and fell asleep after taking several tranquilizers. Later that evening he awakened and proceeded upstairs where Mrs. Wernert was watching television in the living room. Arterberry stopped to pet the dog and had second thoughts about following through with the murders. As he made his way to the door to leave, he was spotted by Mrs. Wernert, so he struck her at least twice with an eighteen-inch crowbar given to him earlier by David Wernert. Arterberry said he intended to leave, but Mrs. Bush came out of her bedroom carrying a flashlight, and he must have struck her several times, although he had no recollection of doing so.[60]

Arterberry said on tape that he ransacked a bedroom to simulate a burglary and took about ten dollars and some jewelry before fleeing.[61] At trial, Arterberry denied killing the women and said that the taped confession was coerced by Detective Stiles's promise to reduce the charges against him.[62]

At David Wernert's trial, prosecutors claimed that he voluntarily assisted in the planning and execution of the murder plot.[63] David Wernert testified that he was a reluctant party to the planning of the murders by his wife and Arterberry and that he took part in the plot only after Arterberry threatened both him and his son.[64] However, David Werner's taped statement was also played and jurors heard him tell authorities that, while he was not enthusiastic about killing the women, their deteriorating physical condition convinced him that it was the proper thing to do. He said that all three codefendants had discussed killing the women and that the following day he took Arterberry to his mother's home on the pretext of removing some tires. He said that the plan called for Arterberry to hide in the house until the Wernerts had established an alibi by having dinner with friends. Arterberry was to then kill the women.[65]

Closing arguments in all three cases were heard on September 20, 1976, just seven days after the trials began. Assistant Prosecutor Robert Gilmer said that Wernert's taped statement to the police showed that she had knowledge of and took part in the murder plans. He added that she also arranged for the Wernerts to have an alibi on the night of the murders.[66] Assistant Prosecutor Bates asserted that Wernert was responsible for the deaths even if the original plan was only to burglarize the house, because the deaths were a foreseeable result of such a plan.[67]

Defense attorney Wysocki challenged the soundness of Wernert's taped statement, claiming that Detective Stiles's interrogation consisted of leading questions asked while she was under the influence of alcohol and tranquilizing drugs. He added that Wernert had no motive to take part in the killings since she was not a direct beneficiary of the victims' wills.[68]

Following closing arguments, jurors in both the Wernerts' trials were instructed to consider only the aggravated murder charges, while Arterberry's jury was told it could also consider the lesser charge of murder without premeditation. The jurors were sequestered and informed that all three verdicts would be announced simultaneously.[69]

On September 21, 1976, following about ten hours of deliberations, Wernert's jury of eight women and four men returned its verdict.[70] Verdicts in the trials of her codefendants had been returned earlier.[71] All three jury verdicts were read minutes apart in their respective courtrooms, which had been locked after being filled beyond capacity with spectators, attorneys, and courthouse personnel who had followed the trials.[72]

Wernert was found guilty of two counts of aggravated murder in the commission of a felony with specifications that the murders were done for hire and that the plan was to kill more than one person. She showed no emotion upon the reading of the verdict and appeared to be resigned to hearing an unfavorable decision. One juror said the members had little trouble arriving at a verdict on the murder charges but that it was more difficult to decide on the multiple deaths specification because of Wernert's testimony that she loved Mrs. Bush and did not want her to be hurt. This same juror said a guilty verdict on the murder-for-hire specification was quickly reached.[73]

David Wernert's jury of eight women and four men took less than three hours to convict him on two counts of aggravated murder with specifications that the murders were done in the commission of a burglary and that the plan was to kill more than one person. He was found innocent of the murder-for-hire specification.[74] Arterberry's jury of four women and eight men deliberated approximately twelve hours[75] before finding him guilty of two counts of aggravated murder with murder-for-hire, multiple deaths, and murder committed during a burglary specifications.[76]

Two months later, on November 22, 1976, Wernert appeared before the judge for sentencing and calmly proclaimed her innocence, adding that she would appeal her conviction. She told the court that she had not received a fair trial in Lucas County in part because her attorney was hindered during voir dire examination of potential jurors. At the hearing, defense attorney Wysocki did not present any evidence of mitigating circumstances which could call for a lesser sentence than the death penalty. He told the court that he could not argue mitigating circumstances for something his client continued to maintain she did not do. Assistant Prosecutor Bates noted that, without mitigating factors to consider, the court was under a statutory obligation to impose the death penalty. Representatives of the court's diagnostic and treatment center and adult probation department also offered testimony as to mitigating factors. No mitigating evidence was found by Judge Glasser, who proceeded to set an April 6, 1977, execution date.[77] Wernert was transported to the Ohio Reformatory for Women in Marysville and placed on death row with Sandra Lockett and Alberta Osborne. David Wernert and Arterberry were also sentenced to death.[78]

Wernert pursued her case on appeal. On May 25, 1979, the court of appeals denied five of her six assignments of error from the verdict and sentence as well as a seventh assignment of error filed in a supplemental brief.[79] Wernert's first assignment of error claimed that the trial court erred in overruling her motion to suppress the taped confession she made to police officers shortly after her arrest. The appellate court held that the confession was voluntary and that the erasure, if not de minimis, was not prejudicial.[80] The second assignment of error argued that the trial court erred in denying the defense's request for an *in camera* inspection of all writings made by the Lucas County coroner and Detective Stiles during the course of their investigations.[81] The appellate court held that such writings by a witness, made for his own use during an investigation, were not required for production under the Ohio Rules of Criminal Procedure.[82]

The third assignment of error asserted that prejudicial error was committed by the trial court in permitting the prosecution's examination of Wernert's religious beliefs through questions pertaining to witchcraft. The appellate court held that the defense had failed to object to this line of testimony at the trial court and thus was precluded from bringing the issue on appeal. The appellate court added that "as to the defendant-appellant being a witch or her interest therein, defendant insinuated this matter into the record on cross-examination of a state witness." The fourth assignment of error claimed that testimony by Detective Stiles as to David Wernert's characterization of the murders as "mercy killings" was hearsay and should not have been admitted by the trial court. The appellate court ruled that Wernert acknowledged and adopted David Wernert's statement when, after being confronted with it, she told Detective Stiles that her prior statement to him was false and that the women had been killed for reasons of mercy. The appellate court reasoned that the statement thus became her own confession by ratification or adoption and was admissible against her.[83]

The fifth assignment of error asserted that the evidence had failed to prove beyond a reasonable doubt that Wernert participated in aggravated burglary.[84] She argued that the evidence presented failed to show a trespass and that in any event she did not trespass in the home of the victims nor strike the fatal blow. The appellate court disagreed, stating that there was ample evidence to establish that she was an active participant in all stages of the conspiracy and thus aware that the occurrence of a homicide was a natural and probable consequence of the common plan.[85] The sixth issue raised by Wernert on appeal was to challenge the constitutionality of Ohio's death penalty statute, an issue that had been decided by the U.S. Supreme Court's ruling in *Lockett v. Ohio*[86] announced ten months earlier.[87] *Lockett* held that the Ohio death penalty statute was unconstitutional, as it prohibited a judge from hearing all mitigating evidence at sentencing.[88] As a result, Wernert was released into the general prison population to serve a life sentence.[89]

The seventh assignment of error alleged that Sergeant Richard Zielinski of the Toledo Police Crime Laboratory, who falsely testified that he possessed a bachelor's degree in pharmacy, committed perjury which denied Wernert due process of law. Sergeant Zielinski had testified for the prosecution that a hammer found at the scene tested positive for either animal or human blood. The appellate court concluded that disclosure of Sergeant Zielinski's perjury would not have produced a different result in the trial, saying, "[W]e do not find the cause of death to be the turning point in this case."[90]

On May 12, 1980, Wernert's first petition for writ of certiorari to the U.S. Supreme Court was denied.[91] Wernert subsequently petitioned the trial court for leave to file a new trial motion based on the grounds of newly discovered evidence, but the trial court denied this motion. On April 23, 1982, the Lucas County Court of Appeals unanimously upheld the trial court's ruling.[92] The newly discovered evidence that Wernert wanted the court to hear was testimony by David Wernert that she had no part in and no actual knowledge of the events leading to the murders. Additionally, Wernert again claimed a denial of due process due to the testimony of Sergeant Zielinski, who had subsequently been indicted for perjury based in part on the testimony given at her trial.[93]

Wernert argued that the trial court erred by denying her request for a new trial when the proposed motion for a new trial had not yet been submitted. The trial court had acknowledged that while only the motion for leave was properly before it, the parties had submitted briefs arguing the merits of a motion for a new trial, and the evidence presented by Wernert was inadequate to grant such a trial.[94] The appellate court found no prejudice to Wernert in the procedure followed by the trial court.[95]

The trial court also found that David Wernert's testimony could not be characterized as newly discovered evidence because it was available and discoverable at the time of Wernert's trial. The appellate court agreed, stating, "Defendant did not make a proffer of this testimony at trial and only conjectures that David Wernert would have asserted his Fifth Amendment privilege against self-incrimination if he had been called as a witness at defendant's trial." Additionally, the appellate court agreed with the trial court that a new trial motion based on Sergeant Zielinski's false testimony was barred by res judicata, contrary to Wernert's assertion that while the issue had been discussed on direct appeal it was not properly before the appellate court. Justice Potter concurred in the judgment but stated his belief that both the trial and appellate courts were limited to ruling on the motion for leave and that it was premature to rule on the merits of a new trial motion.[96]

On December 13, 1983, Wernert filed a petition for postconviction relief, which was dismissed by the Lucas County Court of Common Pleas. On October 19, 1984, the Lucas County Court of Appeals unanimously affirmed the trial court's decision. Wernert claimed two assignments of error on appeal. She alleged that evidence favorable to her defense was improperly withheld by the prosecution and that jury instructions issued at her trial relieved the prosecution of proving the essential element of intent beyond a reasonable doubt. The first assignment of error involved a scientific report regarding hair samples taken from the victims. The appellate court held that "broad assertions" calling this report exculpatory were insufficient to justify a full-blown postconviction hearing under Ohio statutory law. As to the second assignment of error, the appellate court found that Wernert's failure to object to the jury instructions at trial and in subsequent appeals rendered the issue res judicata, precluding later objection to them.[97]

Wernert then proceeded into federal court. She sought a writ of habeas corpus from the federal district court, alleging violations of her Fifth and Sixth Amendment rights and claiming that perjured testimony rendered her trial fundamentally unfair. The district court denied the writ, and Wernert appealed to the Sixth Circuit Court of Appeals.[98] At the Sixth Circuit, for the first time in the appellate process, Wernert found a sympathetic ear in one judge who agreed that the interrogation following her arrest was in violation of her right to counsel. District Judge Enslen, sitting by designation, cast a lone dissenting vote as the Sixth Circuit affirmed the district court's ruling two to one.[99]

Wernert presented the Sixth Circuit with a three-pronged collateral attack upon her conviction. First, she asserted that the incriminating statements she made on tape were improperly obtained after she had expressed a desire to consult with an attorney and thus should have been suppressed at trial. Second, she argued that the admission into evidence of her husband's confession violated her Sixth Amendment right to confront witnesses against her. Third, she claimed that the perjured testimony of Sergeant Zielinski offered by the prosecution rendered the trial fundamentally unfair.[100]

The Sixth Circuit denied the first prong of Wernert's attack, finding that her statement to the jail matron that her husband would telephone their attorney, as well as her own unannounced effort to call an attorney, were not enough to put authorities on notice that she intended to retract her waiver of her Miranda rights and invoke her right to counsel. The Sixth Circuit noted that Wernert had been read her rights three times and had repeatedly waived them, stating, "Invocation of the right to counsel, to be effective, must be communicated; and as we read this record, the police were not apprised that Mrs. Wernert had changed her mind and wanted to consult with counsel."[101] Judge Enslen dissented based upon his belief that Wernert adequately informed the authorities of her desire to consult with counsel, stating:

> [M]y reading of the record is that the police were aware of appellant's belief that her husband would call an attorney. Detective Stiles testified at the state court suppression hearing that he was present when the Matron asked appellant if she would like to call her attorney. Although this point is not clear from the record, presumably if Detective Stiles heard the Matron's question, then he also heard the appellant's reply. At that point, he at least should have inquired further into appellant's desire to have counsel present. His failure to do so and to respect appellant's expression of her desire to seek the assistance of counsel rendered his subsequent questioning of her invalid.[102]

The Sixth Circuit also rejected Wernert's argument that any waiver of her right to counsel was not made intelligently and voluntarily due to the effects of drugs and alcohol, concern about the welfare of her son, lack of sleep and sustenance, and inexperience with law enforcement. The Sixth Circuit cited expert testimony which indicated that the effects of the drugs and alcohol would have peaked at noon on the day before she endorsed her husband's account of the murder. Additionally, the court stated that Wernert had been told by the police that her son was being cared for in a children's home and that her lack of sustenance could not have been too serious an impairment since she had eaten dinner the night before the statements were made. As to Wernert's contention that inexperience with law enforcement procedure impaired her ability to properly waive her rights, the Sixth Circuit replied that the "repeated painstaking enumeration of her rights" rendered such an assertion "unavailing."[103]

The Sixth Circuit denied the second prong of Wernert's attack, holding that her right of confrontation was not violated by the admission of testimony that she had endorsed her husband's out-of-court confession.[104] Citing *Poole v. Perini*,[105] the court stated, "An adoptive confession avoids the confrontation problem because the words of the hearsay become the words of the defendant." Attempting to distinguish her case from *Poole,* Wernert argued that her endorsement of her husband's confession was unreliable because she was "coerced" into it as a result of their marital relationship. The Sixth Circuit rejected this argument, stating, "The relationship is irrelevant, in our view; Mrs. Wernert has never alleged that she endorsed her husband's statement out of fear that she would do her husband harm by contradicting him. On the contrary, she has consistently denied ever having said that her husband's statement was correct."[106]

The Sixth Circuit also rejected the third prong of Wernert's attack, holding that there was no reasonable likelihood that the false testimony of Sergeant Zielinski could have influenced the jury's verdict. Wernert contended that because the type of weapon used is material to a determination of whether or not a murder was committed purposely, Sergeant Zielinski's testimony that either human or animal blood was present on a hammer found in the victim's home, coupled with the coroner's implication that this hammer was the murder weapon, may have influenced the jury in its finding of purposefulness. The Sixth Circuit disagreed, stating:

> Whether the hammer found in the victims' basement was or was not the murder weapon is irrelevant to a finding of purposefulness here. . . . The coroner testified that the victim died of "multiple blows" to the skull, and that the blows "actually pulverized the skull in the area with depression into the brain substance itself." He opined that the velocity of the blows was "significant" and that the weapon was of "significant weight." The person who wielded the weapon could hardly be thought to have been acting absent-mindedly.[107]

The Sixth Circuit added that since the prosecution did not claim that Wernert herself wielded the weapon but merely that she had planned the murders carried out by Arterberry, a finding as to whether Arterberry acted purposely in inflicting the blows had no bearing on the purposefulness of her actions.[108] On January 11, 1988, the U.S. Supreme Court again denied Wernert's petition for writ of certiorari.[109]

Wernert continued to maintain that she should have received a lesser sentence based on the fact that she was not present at the scene of the crime and did not take part in the killings. "I had never been in any type of trouble before and at that time had no real knowledge or understanding of criminal law and such things as plea bargaining," she explained in a 1990 letter to the author. "I believed with all my heart that I was not guilty of killing anyone and felt that surely my trial would clearly prove this." Wernert added that "fear," "psychological trauma," and "disorientation" resulting from her pretrial incarceration rendered her ineffective in assisting her attorneys in the preparation of a defense.[110]

Like Lockett and Osborne, Wernert did not directly participate in killing the victims involved. Wernert's mother-in-law and grandmother-in-law were brutally beaten to death with a crowbar by an acquaintance of Wernert and her husband.[111] The victims were sixty-seven and ninety-six at the time of their deaths,[112] and the apparent motive was monetary.[113] The outrage and public interest in the murder of these two women is demonstrated by the volume of information available on the murders. Unlike the previous cases, there are few or no peculiar circumstances outside of the murders which would have placed Wernert in an unfavorable light. Her sheer greed may be her most repulsive characteristic.

THIRTEEN

Benita Smith

Sentenced in 1977, Reversed in 1978

ON SEPTEMBER 11, 1977, Benita Smith was convicted of aggravated murder in the shooting death of a businessman.[1] In November, Smith was sentenced to die by electrocution.[2] Smith did not personally commit the murder for which she was charged.[3] Instead, prosecutors claimed that Smith aided her brother in a robbery that led to murder.[4] Smith and her brother were tried separately but simultaneously in the Lucas County Common Pleas Court.[5]

Smith was twenty-three years old at the time of her arrest, and her brother a mere twenty.[6] They were accused of the robbery-murder of Jules Vinnedge, the operations manager of a store, who was shot in the head on May 3, 1977, while he was en route to make a bank deposit of more than $4,000.[7]

Forty prospective jurors were slated for examination in each of the trials and were to be questioned separately in both cases.[8] Jurors were taken to the shopping center parking lot to view the scene of the crime before the prosecution presented its evidence.[9] In its opening statement, the prosecution asserted that, although her brother had pulled the trigger, Smith was a "major force" behind the robbery that led to the murder and that she "not only aided and abetted her brother in the crime but was also a prime motivating force behind this most heinous act in which Jules Vinnedge's life was taken." The attorney for the defense noted that the case was "messed up" and that there were "too many details that don't make sense."[10]

The prosecution contended that Smith recruited two friends to drive one of the two cars that took the defendants to the murder scene. After her brother shot the victim, Smith yelled, "Get the bag! Get the bag!" Her brother retrieved the bag, and they fled in one of the cars. They later switched cars, leaving one at a carryout. Afterward, Smith asked a friend if she would drive to pick up the car they had left behind. Witnesses also saw Smith attempting to burn the bank bag that had been stolen from the victim.[11]

Testimony at trial was inconclusive as to the identification of Smith and her brother. Three persons at the scene of the crime were unable to identify Smith's brother as a suspect, two witnesses were unable to identify any of several men in a lineup, and one witness identified someone other than Smith's brother.[12] Other statements from witnesses variously indicated that the suspect wore a scarf, a wide-brimmed hat, a stocking cap, and nothing on his head.[13]

Testimony that led to the conviction of Smith was primarily from three witnesses: two sisters who drove one of the two cars used in the commission of the crime and an acquaintance to whom Smith offered money to "drive a car on a job." The two sisters, ages fifteen and seventeen, testified that they had known Smith and her brother for about a week when Smith asked if they would drive her to the store. The older sister agreed, and Smith's brother drove another car to a carryout. Smith told the sisters that she and her brother were going to go to the store and "steal a rack of clothes." The sisters did not want to get into trouble, so they waited at the carryout while Smith and her brother drove off in the other car. After forty-five minutes to an hour, Smith and her brother drove up to the carryout with "a screech of tires." Smith and her brother, who was clutching a blue bank bag to his chest, ran and got into the car the sisters were driving. Smith's brother crouched on the rear floor and Smith lay on the rear seat while telling the girls, "Hurry up and get out of here." Once they all arrived home, Smith gave both girls $50 and said, "That's for being cool." Smith then asked the younger sister if she knew someone who would retrieve the other car. The younger sister and her friends drove to the carryout to retrieve the car, but it had been towed by police. The sister and her friends were stopped and questioned and later released after telling police that an unknown woman had given them the car keys and asked them to retrieve the car. Once the older sister found out about the murder, she went to the police. She told the authorities how Smith had burned the bank bag stolen from the victim by dousing it with lighter fluid on an upside-down trash lid.[14] This action was also witnessed by another sister who testified at trial.[15] The ashes, the bag's zipper, and the trash lid were all introduced as evidence at trial.[16]

An acquaintance testified that Smith offered him money "to drive a car on a job" on the same morning that the victim was killed. He said that she offered him $200 to drive the car to an unspecified location and to wait for her and another $500 once the task was completed. He said he refused the offer. He also testified that he saw a loaded pistol at Smith's home on the day of the shooting that was similar in appearance to the murder weapon. He testified that he also heard Smith tell her brother that the gun would not be necessary and that the brother then put the gun back in a closet in Smith's home.[17]

Other testimony included that of a store clerk who said that the store's deposit procedure was known by several persons and that it would have been easy for others to find out about it because of its regularity. Ballistic and fingerprint experts from the Ohio Bureau of Criminal Identification also testified.[18] Defense attorneys focused on the absence of certain tests, most particularly those for fingerprints on the car allegedly driven by Smith during the crime and that to determine whether Smith's brother had materials on his hand that would indicate he had fired a weapon.[19] There was also inconsistency between the coroner's report, which stated that the victim was killed with a .32-caliber bullet, and testimony from the ballistics expert that the victim was killed by a 9-mm bullet from Smith's semiautomatic pistol.[20] Smith's sister-in-law also testified that Smith had borrowed her car and that, once Smith realized that it had been seized by the police, Smith suggested that the sister-in-law report that it had been stolen, which she refused to do.[21]

Closing arguments began after the defense presented only one witness in its case, a man who was arrested in the murder prior to the Smiths and then released once his alibi proved valid. In closing argument, the defense attorney asserted that the state had numerous conflicts in the testimony of its thirty-plus witnesses. He particularly attacked the credibility of the testimony of the two sisters. The prosecutor found the defense's arguments to be "preposterous" and claimed that Smith "not only aided and abetted her brother" but was "the principal planner and cover-upper." He pointed at Smith as he told the jury to look at the actions of her brother "as if this defendant were crouched on his shoulder." Near the end of his argument, the prosecutor became faint and was taken to the hospital and released. After a short recess, another prosecutor completed the rebuttal argument. The judge gave the jury instructions before the jurors retired for the night. Although a verdict had already been reached in Smith's brother's case, his jury remained sequestered and the verdict sealed during Smith's jury deliberations.[22]

After four and one-half hours of deliberation, the jury returned a unanimous guilty verdict on the charge of aggravated murder, which included a specification that the murder had occurred during a robbery. Smith's brother was convicted of the same offense. Smith's attorneys requested a directed verdict of acquittal, which was denied.[23]

On November 30, 1977, Smith was sentenced to death after a mitigation hearing in which the judge ruled that he could not find sufficient evidence to support mitigation of the death penalty. Smith had nothing to say to the court before she was sentenced, but she did take the stand under oath in her mitigation hearing. She testified that she had been using drugs the night before the robbery. She claimed a store detective gave her the idea for the robbery. She said that she had told her brother that the gun was not necessary and that she did not know he had the gun until she saw him pull it out when the victim resisted handing over the bank bag.[24]

In 1978, when the U.S. Supreme Court ruled in *Lockett v. Ohio* that the Ohio death penalty statute was unconstitutional because it prohibited a judge from hearing all mitigating evidence at sentencing,[25] Smith was released into the general prison population to serve a life sentence.[26] On February 16, 1979, the court of appeals affirmed Smith's conviction, finding her assignments of error either moot or not well taken.[27] Smith's life sentence entitled her to a hearing before the commutation board at the fifteen-year mark, in 1992. While incarcerated, Smith "has gone through a number of severe psychological changes and at one time was probated to the mental forensic unit in Columbus for several months." She also has other health problems, including problems with her heart, and at times requires hospitalization.[28]

Smith did not kill the victim but instead acted as an accomplice to her brother, who did kill the victim during the course of a robbery.[29] Smith did, however, demonstrate a complete disregard for life and law through her actions. She made use of minors in the plot and she carried out the well-thought-out plan without hesitation. By giving the minors money "for being cool" and referring to the plan as a "job,"[30] Smith also demonstrated that she was comfortable and confident in her actions and acted as if she had been involved in similar acts for years. The sources reveal little personal information about Smith, and from the acts described, one can get only a sense of how pure her aggression was.

Sharon Faye Young

Sentenced in 1983, Reversed in 1986

SHARON FAYE Young was sentenced to death when she murdered and robbed a bar owner.[1] On June 11, 1983, Young and some women friends, who were all homosexual, went to a gay bar in Cincinnati. Young had been drinking that night and continued to drink at the bar.[2] At one point during the evening, she went behind the bar under the pretense of making a phone call. While she was behind the bar, another customer prevented her from taking money from the cash register. Although Young was unable to obtain any money, she did take a gun that the victim kept near the cash register.[3] The customer related his observations to the victim, who then "patted down" Young and was satisfied that she had not taken any money. The victim then noticed his gun was missing, but Young protested her innocence, and the gun, which was hidden in her pocket, was not discovered. Both Young and the victim appeared very intoxicated to other customers in the bar. The victim was observed kissing Young and fondling her breasts, and he told other customers that Young had consented to "go to bed with him."[4] At closing time, Young left with the victim in his car. She informed him that she was going to rob him and instructed him to drive to a deserted area. After he pulled over to the side of the road, she shot him.[5]

While the exact circumstances surrounding the shooting are unclear, it was shown at trial that the victim was shot once in the back of the head. After killing the victim, Young took his wallet and left the scene in his car. Young was arrested in Columbus two days later. She was still driving the victim's car, from which the gun used in the murder was recovered.[6]

On July 5, 1983, the grand jury returned a two-count indictment charging Young with aggravated robbery with a firearm specification and aggravated murder with the specification that the offense was committed for the purpose of escaping detection, apprehension, trial, or punishment, that the offense was committed during an aggravated robbery, and that Young was the principal offender. Young pleaded not guilty to the charges, and trial commenced on September 6, 1983.[7] Young did not testify at her trial, but she gave a taped statement in which she admitted to robbing the victim and shooting him in the course of the robbery. She maintained, however, that she did not intend to kill him.[8] The jury returned verdicts of guilty to all charges and the specifications on September 14, 1983. The mitigation hearing commenced on September 17, 1983, and the jury returned its recommendation to impose the death penalty the following day. The trial court, on September 30, 1983, adopted the jury's recommendation of death. The trial court imposed the death sentence as to the charge of aggravated murder, alternatively imposing a sentence of life imprisonment without parole for thirty years in the event that the death penalty was set aside. Additionally, the trial court imposed three years of actual incarceration for the firearm specification of the aggravated robbery charge and seven to twenty-five years of incarceration on the aggravated robbery charge.[9]

Young appealed her conviction, assigning ten errors. Young stated that the trial court erred by refusing to instruct the jury on the lesser included offense of involuntary manslaughter and on the issue of intoxication, by denying her motions for mistrial based on the prosecution's misconduct and the jury's return of improper verdict forms, and by ruling that the aggravating circumstances outweighed the mitigating factors. Further, Young alleged error in not allowing her to exercise her final peremptory challenge, in allowing the state to argue first and last during closing arguments of the penalty phase, in overruling her motion to dismiss based on the unconstitutionality of the Ohio statutes on the imposition of the death penalty, in allowing the prosecution to argue about the "future dangerousness" of Young, and in instructing the jury that the verdict had to be "just to the people who live in this community."[10] Two of Young's assignments of error were well taken.[11]

On the error concerning involuntary manslaughter, the Ohio Supreme Court determined that evidence on the kind and amount of intoxicants that Young consumed, coupled with the opinions expressed by the state's witnesses as to Young's intoxication, compelled the giving of the involuntary manslaughter instruction. Also, Young's recorded statement, placed into evidence by the state, indicated that she had not intended to kill the victim but only to take his money.[12] The court ruled that from the record a trier of fact could accept the evidence of Young's intoxication and statement and, thereby, reasonably find against the state and for Young on the element of purpose to kill.[13]

On the error concerning intoxication, the court noted that Ohio law provided that intoxication is recognized as an affirmative defense and that a special jury charge on the effect of intoxication on the formation of criminal intent is appropriate when that issue is properly raised by the evidence.[14] After considering all the evidence relating to intoxication, the court determined that there was sufficient evidence introduced which, if believed, could raise a question in the minds of reasonable persons concerning whether Young was so intoxicated that her ability to form criminal intent was affected. The court then held that the failure to instruct on intoxication was an abuse of discretion rising to prejudicial error.[15]

The court agreed with Young on elements of her assignment of error concerning misconduct by the prosecution.[16] It perceived misconduct in some of the prosecutor's remarks, ruling that some of the prosecutor's arguments were "totally incorrect and . . . [that it was] at a loss as to how he could utter such remarks."[17] However, the court overruled the assignment of error, determining that the trial court became cognizant of the effect on the jury of the prosecutor's misstatements of law and "cured" the error.[18] The rest of Young's assignments of error were also overruled.[19] Because the court found error in the guilt phase of the trial but not in the penalty phase, it reversed Young's conviction and sentence of death and remanded the cause for a new trial.[20]

The jury in the second trial found Young guilty of aggravated robbery and death-eligible aggravated murder, but it did not recommend the imposition of capital punishment. Young was accordingly ordered to serve a life term in prison with parole eligibility after thirty years.[21] Young also appealed this second conviction and sentencing, alleging error by the trial court in failing to grant her motion for mistrial based on the prosecution's misconduct, in instructing that it was Young's burden to establish intoxication by a preponderance of the evidence, in not dismissing the second count of the indictment, in not finding the jury's verdict against the weight of the evidence, and in failing to grant a motion for acquittal.[22]

The court agreed that the prosecutor's conduct was "improvident" but found the error to be harmless, noting that the trial court had ruled at the time that the prosecutor's conduct was not prejudicial and gave appropriate limiting instructions to the jury. The court found all other errors to be without merit and overruled them as well.[23] The judgment of the trial court in the second trial, of life imprisonment with parole eligibility after thirty years, was affirmed.[24]

Like Smith, Young could be described as having no regard for life or law. The factor of intoxication,[25] however, seems to lessen the hardness of Young's persona. One must wonder how she would have acted if she had not been intoxicated. Young left the bar with the bar owner under the pretense of having sex with him[26] but then shot him in the back of the head once they reached a deserted area.[27] That the shot was to the back of the head suggests an execution, and the damage to her case was compounded by Young's monetary motive.[28] Other than Young's homosexuality,[29] there appears to be little else in terms of circumstances or characteristics that would have affected the jury's decision.

FIFTEEN

Rosalie Grant

Sentenced in 1983, Commuted in 1991

ROSALIE GRANT was twenty-three years old when she was convicted of killing two of her three children by setting a fire in her home in Youngstown.[1] Grant was accused of spraying her two sons, ages two years and eleven months, with charcoal lighter fluid as they slept in their beds and setting them on fire on April 1, 1983.[2] Grant's three-year-old daughter escaped injury, as she was spending the night with her grandmother.[3] The alleged motive was to collect on $5,000 life insurance policies taken out on each of her sons just a few weeks earlier.[4] Grant did not take out a policy on her daughter.[5]

Grant maintained her innocence throughout all the proceedings of her case.[6] Her story was that she put the boys to bed and that around 1:00 A.M.

she dozed off in front of the television. She woke up, smelling smoke in the room, ran through the house, and saw black smoke pouring through the crack of the closed door of the children's bedroom. She froze for a second in terror as she heard the sounds of her children screaming. She tried repeatedly to enter the bedroom but couldn't move through the flames. She then phoned the fire department and ran outside for help.[7] By the time the fire department arrived, they were too late to save the boys. Apparently, the older boy had tried to crawl toward the door, and the baby was thrown to the floor when his crib burned and collapsed.[8] Coroner's reports indicated the boys did not suffocate from the smoke but were burned to death.[9]

The prosecution maintained that there were too many coincidences for the deaths to have been accidental and that the fatal fire was deliberately set. Arson and insurance investigators testified that the flames were confined to the children's room and that a fire accelerant was used to set the fire. Remnants of four or five separate fires in the basement indicated Grant tried to burn the whole house down, the prosecution asserted. Traces of a substance identical to charcoal lighter fluid in the fuse box signified Grant's effort to make it appear as if an electrical malfunction touched off the fire. Grant's fingerprints were found on a can of lighter fluid even though she did not own a barbecue grill. The prosecution stated that Grant had a motive, the life insurance money, and means, the lighter fluid.[10]

The defense counsel called the prosecution's case a "castle of sand," and then, even more emphatically, a "persecution, not a prosecution." Defense counsel maintained that Grant was the victim of an overzealous, incomplete investigation by both fire officials and police officers. The defense tried to show that the insurance money was not a motive, that there were no witnesses who could identify Grant as the arsonist, and that a fire department tape demonstrated that Grant was hysterical on the day of the fire.[11]

In a brief rebuttal, the prosecution picked up the fire department tape and called it the "fatal flaw" in the defense's case. He said that testimony showed Grant had never tried to enter the children's room that night because there was too much smoke and heat. He then pointed out that, on the tape, Grant clearly screamed that her children were on fire. The prosecutor asked, "How could she know that if she never opened the door? I'll tell you how. She was the one that set that fire and closed the door behind her."[12]

On October 14, 1983, after deliberating almost nine hours over two days, the jury of nine men and three women came back with a verdict of guilty on two counts of aggravated murder and one count of aggravated arson. As the judge read the verdict, Grant and several family members wept quietly.[13] One week later, on October 21, 1983, at Grant's mitigation hearing, defense counsel brought up as mitigating factors Grant's young age, troubled family background, and lack of a prior criminal record. He maintained that Grant did not pose a danger to society. He also suggested that she was a good candidate for rehabilitation and asked the jury to consider the impact of her execution upon her surviving three-year-old daughter.[14] Grant also made an unsworn statement over an hour long on her own behalf. This statement "sealed her own fate," opined her attorneys and the prosecution. Grant maintained her innocence, stated that a man wielding a pipe prevented her from entering her children's room, and told the jurors they made a mistake by convicting her and that they would be murderers if they recommended the death penalty. She also intimated that the all-white jury exhibited racial bias when it found her guilty.[15] "For the first ten minutes, some of the members of the jury had tears in their eyes," the prosecutor remembered, and "if she had stopped there, things might have been all right." Grant wept as she talked, but then her voice became harsh, angry, whining, and accusative. "It reminded me of someone scratching their fingernails on a blackboard," the prosecutor stated. "It surely didn't do her any good," her attorney remarked.[16]

The jury unanimously decided that the aggravating factors that resulted in conviction sufficiently outweighed any factors for a lesser penalty. Under Ohio law, the jury had to recommend the death penalty.[17] Afterward, when the court polled the jurors individually on the verdicts, they did not look at Grant or her attorneys.[18] The judge retired to his chambers to review the findings and the evidence as required by law before pronouncing sentence. He could have reduced the death penalty to twenty or thirty years imprisonment. After twenty minutes, he returned to the bench, said that it was his duty to accept the recommendation of the jury, and sentenced Grant to death for the aggravated murder charges. He also sentenced her to seven to twenty-five years for the arson charge.[19]

The Office of the Ohio Public Defender pursued the weaknesses of the case against Grant. It asserted that the only evidence was the $5,000 life insurance policies, Grant's fingerprints on a can of charcoal lighter fluid, and Grant's presence in the house when the fire started. The prosecution apparently never established that the fire was started with the charcoal lighter fluid. Further, Grant had given birth to her youngest son just eleven months before the incident. Facts were present in the record to indicate that she may have suffered from postpartum psychosis at the time of the fire, but no effort was made at trial to determine whether she did, in fact, have this condition. The defense claimed to have been shocked at Grant's guilty verdict.[20]

Grant appealed her conviction and sentencing, alleging thirty-five assignments of error.[21] These errors included assertions of improperly admitted evidence obtained from warrantless searches, admissions of prior bad acts, the lack of an independent, underlying felony, qualification of certain witnesses to testify as experts, failure to grant motions and continuances requested by the defense, incorrect jury instructions, and questions on the constitutionality of the death penalty statutes. While finding that a few of her errors had merit, the court ruled these errors were harmless.[22] The court found Grant's age, twenty-two at the time of the offense, and her prior employment history, which consisted in part of the care of handicapped and retarded children, to be of some weight in mitigation.[23] However, the court found beyond a reasonable doubt that the aggravating circumstances outweighed the mitigating evidence.[24] The court then ruled the sentence of death appropriate in Grant's case, and on November 9, 1990, it affirmed the judgment of the lower court.[25]

Nearly three years later, the Ohio Supreme Court reviewed the same appeal.[26] This court also rejected all thirty-five alleged errors as being either insignificant or incorrectly alleged.[27] Discussing mitigation, the court agreed that Grant had had a difficult life, remarking:

> She witnessed the stabbing death of her stepfather at the hand of her mother. Her abusive mother threatened her with death, and saw Grant and her sisters as a way to receive welfare funds. Grant has little education and was seldom employed. However, Grant had a good relationship with her paternal grandmother. She lived virtually rent-free in a house owned by her grandmother. Her relationship with her father was fairly close, and she had a good number of friends. Life could have been much worse for Rosalie Grant.[28]

In reference to the appropriateness of her sentence, the court maintained that "the nature and circumstances of the offense provide no mitigating features. Rosalie Grant burned her children alive. . . . In this case the crime committed was so severe, its abhorrent nature so apparent, that nothing in Grant's past mitigates against our applying the maximum punishment allowed by law."[29] Grant's continued denial raised a level of residual doubt, but her lack of remorse in her presentence unsworn statement removed remorse as a possible "other factor."[30] In regard to other factors to be considered, the court admitted that much of their residual doubt came from their reluctance to "believe anyone could commit such an awful crime, much less the children's mother."[31] The judgment of the court of appeals was affirmed on October 27, 1993.[32] On December 15, 1993, the Ohio Supreme Court denied a motion for a rehearing.[33]

On January 10, 1991, Governor Richard Celeste, in one of his last official acts before leaving office, commuted to life in prison the death sentences of eight prisoners, including Grant and three other women who were then on death row.[34] There was much opposition to the commutations, especially from the attorney general and the incoming governor, who urged the court to rescind the commutations.[35] They stated that Governor Celeste had failed to follow Ohio law, which required an application for commutation to the Adult Parole Authority and an investigation by the parole board.[36] On February 13, 1992, the court of common pleas ruled that the pardons and commutations were "null and void"[37] and reinstated the death sentences of the prisoners, including Grant.[38] In 1994, the court of appeals reversed the decision of the court of common pleas, stating that "neither the constitution nor the statute" limited the governor's power to grant pardons and that "the wisdom and merits of such actions are not for consideration of the courts."[39]

Grant is one of only two women in Ohio to have received a death sentence for the murder of her own children. Evidence that Grant had tried numerous times to start the fire and that the boys actually died from being burned and not from smoke inhalation generated anger toward her.[40] It was also damaging that Grant had insurance, which was newly acquired, only on the two boys and not on her daughter, who was not at home at the time of the fire.[41] The sources indicate that Grant actually sealed her own fate during her mitigation hearing when she transitioned from being a weeping mother into an angry defendant.[42] The factors of her troubled childhood, young age, past employment providing care for handicapped and retarded children, and surviving daughter were not enough to keep Grant from being sentenced to death.[43]

SIXTEEN

Debra Brown

Sentenced in 1985, Commuted in 1991

DEBRA BROWN was just twenty years old when she took part in the murder for which she was sentenced to death. Brown's common-law husband, Alton Coleman, also was charged and convicted in connection with the slaying.[1] Both Brown and Coleman were sentenced to death "in connection with a bloody Midwest crime spree in 1984 that sent shock waves through six states" and left eight people dead. Coleman was convicted of four murders and sentenced to death in four states, including Ohio. His sentence was not affected by Governor Richard Celeste's decision to commute the sentences of eight prisoners, including that of Brown.[2]

On the morning of July 11, 1984, Tonnie Storey, the fifteen-year-old black victim, left her home to attend a summer school class. Storey never returned home.[3] She was last seen with Coleman and a woman matching Brown's description.[4] On July 19, 1984, a partially decomposed body, later identified through fingerprints as that of Storey, was discovered in an abandoned building. Storey's death was determined to be a homicide.[5] The victim's clothing was found near a footprint identical to one found at another murder scene. Both prints were later discovered to have been made by shoes worn by Coleman. Other evidence also implicated Coleman.[6]

Brown and Coleman were indicted on two counts of aggravated murder and one count of aggravated robbery. The two counts of aggravated murder contained specifications of aggravating circumstances that would justify the imposition of capital punishment.[7]

Brown grew up in an extremely abusive home with an alcoholic and mentally ill father.[8] One defense attorney for her appeal, after going to Brown's hometown of Gary, Indiana, to investigate her family life, stated that "there [were] no words to describe what [he] saw." He said that "[i]t was less than poverty and that anything [he said] would be inadequate." He maintained that "condemned buildings, rats, holes in walls and worries about where the next meal would come from were part of the daily routine." His opinion was that "[i]f a jury could have understood all of that, they would never have sent her to the chair."[9]

At first, Brown took the blame for the murder entirely upon herself, but she was "weaned away from this protectiveness" of her husband in the course of her legal proceedings.[10] She then contended that she was acting under the dominion of her husband at the time of the crime[11] in an effort to mitigate her punishment.[12] Her relationship with Coleman was characterized by experts as a master-slave relationship.[13] In her appeal, Brown stated that she participated in the crimes solely out of fear of her husband and to prove she loved him; but, at the time of trial, she stated that she believed that his brutal love was the only valuable thing in her life. Supposedly, the manipulative Coleman persuaded her to play the evil woman in her testimony at his trial.[14]

Brown's test results showed an IQ score ranging from 59 to 74, a classification of retarded and learning disabled. Her passive-dependent personality disorder, coupled with retardation, may have led to Coleman's control of her. A psychologist reported that Brown's tests all revealed themes of childlike emotional development, excessive reliance on others, and susceptibility to manipulation by others. He stated that Brown's was the most extreme case of dependency he had ever encountered. Brown had no criminal record before her association with Coleman.[15]

At trial, the state introduced evidence that Brown murdered or participated in the murders of Storey and five other victims and participated in the assaults of or attempts to kill five others.[16] Brown was tried separately by a jury and found guilty on all three counts, with specifications.[17] In the mitigation phase of the trial, the jury determined that the aggravating circumstances of which they had found Brown guilty outweighed the mitigating factors, and it recommended that she be sentenced to death. The trial judge, also finding that the aggravating circumstances of which Brown had been found guilty outweighed the mitigating factors, sentenced Brown to death.[18]

Brown appealed to the First District Court of Appeals of Ohio as an appeal of right.[19] She presented fourteen assignments of error, alleging unconstitutionality of the Ohio capital punishment statutes, an inadequate indictment, prejudice from the refusal of a joint trial, improper denial of a voir dire examination, improper denial of a motion to suppress, and failure to require timely discovery. She also alleged prejudice through the effort to link her to other crimes committed, insufficient evidence, abuse of discretion in denying a motion for a change of venue, prosecutorial misconduct, use of two offenses when only one death occurred, erroneous jury instructions, and ineffective assistance of counsel.[20] The court considered each assignment of error and concluded that none had merit.[21] It then affirmed the judgment of the trial court.[22]

In June 1988, Brown appealed to the Ohio Supreme Court on an appeal as a matter of right.[23] Her assignments of error were facially and substantially similar to those presented to the appeals court.[24] Again, the court upheld her convictions and sentence of death and affirmed the judgment of the lower court, finding that the aggravating circumstances outweighed the mitigating circumstances. Also, pursuant to its statutory duty, the court assessed the imposition of the death penalty as not disproportionate or excessive when compared with other cases in which the death penalty had been imposed.[25] On October 8, 1988, a motion for a rehearing was denied by the Supreme Court of Ohio.[26]

On April 17, 1989, Brown's petition for a rehearing was denied by the U.S. Supreme Court.[27] On June 7, 1990, a mandamus petition after attorneys' funds were exhausted pursuant to a contract with the state public defender was dismissed in the Tenth District Court of Appeals, which held that Brown had adequate remedy at law by requesting approval of additional funds from the trial court.[28]

Just as with Rosalie Grant, Brown's sentence was commuted to life in prison by Governor Richard Celeste on January 10, 1991. Unlike Grant, however, Brown did not have the possibility of parole.[29] The attorney who had prosecuted Brown called the governor's decision "a tragedy and an outrage," and Indiana prosecutors sought custody of Brown because she was also sentenced to death in that state for the murder of a seven-year-old girl and the attempted murder and molestation of the girl's nine-year-old aunt.[30] Brown is now serving life in prison without parole in Ohio, but she remains under a sentence of death in Indiana.[31]

Because of Brown's dependency upon Coleman and Coleman's control over Brown,[32] whether Brown or Coleman actually committed the murders is uncertain. What has been determined, however, is that there were multiple female victims.[33] These were apparently targeted at random and killed for no reason other than the gratification one might receive from killing another.

Like postpartum illness (possibly indicated in the case of Rosalie Grant; see chapter 15 supra), Brown's retardation and learning disability might have resulted in a different sentence for her today. At the time of trial, however, Brown's mental disability,[34] troubled childhood,[35] dependency,[36] and manipulation[37] were not enough to keep her from a sentence of death.

SEVENTEEN

Elizabeth Green

Sentenced in 1988, Commuted in 1991

ELIZABETH GREEN was twenty-four years old at the time of the commission of her crime, murder with the intent to rob the victim in order to purchase drugs. The victim was a neighbor of Green's friend and codefendant, Belinda Coulter. Because Coulter testified for the state, she was sentenced on manslaughter charges, despite the fact that she had reaped the benefits of the crime.[1] As a condition of her plea bargain, Coulter received a twelve-year to fifty-year prison term after pleading guilty to involuntary manslaughter and aggravated robbery and then testifying against Green.[2]

Green was found to have an IQ of 66 and can be classified as mentally retarded.[3] She was also developmentally impaired. Green was "abandoned and abused throughout much of her childhood." When she was young, she and her sisters were tied to chairs by their mother, who then set the house on fire. Green was "extremely dependent and easily manipulated." Some suggested that Coulter took advantage of Green's mental disability in order to get her to commit the crime and that Green would not have committed the crime if she had acted alone.[4]

On January 4, 1988, Green went to visit her friend Coulter.[5] Apparently, the two wanted to acquire some cocaine, but neither had enough money to make a purchase. Green suggested that she sell $40 worth of food stamps, and Coulter indicated that her neighbor, Tommie Willis, the seventy-year-old victim, would be willing to buy them. Once that transaction had been completed and the cocaine was purchased and used, the two decided they wanted more cocaine. They came up with a plan to rob and kill Willis because Coulter had noticed that he had a large quantity of cash on him. Coulter and Green went to Willis's residence with socks on their hands so as to leave no prints. They asked Willis to sell them liquor in order to gain entrance into his home.[6] Once they were all inside, Willis became suspicious and produced a knife to protect himself. Green wrestled with Willis and managed to take the knife from him. Then, while yelling for Coulter's assistance, Green stabbed Willis numerous times in the neck and chest. Coulter then also proceeded to stab Willis repeatedly. After inflicting approximately one hundred wounds and thrusting a pillow into Willis's face, Coulter searched his pockets and found a large sum of cash. Prior to leaving the apartment, the women pocketed the money, took the phone off the hook, turned the television off, and removed a bottle of liquor from the kitchen. They then returned to Coulter's residence where they attempted to wash away and dispose of any incriminating evidence.[7]

After three weeks of investigation, Green and Coulter became the focus of the police investigation.[8] Several factors were considered. A bloody child's sock left at the scene suggested that one of the killers had children. Coulter had two children. Two distinct blood types were found at the scene, indicating that one of the killers had been cut. Green had a deep cut on her hand. A shoe print in a small size of seven or seven-and-one-half was found. Coulter wore a size seven. Also, Coulter, who had been without funds prior to the murder, was later seen with a large amount of cash.[9] On the strength of these facts, the police arrested the two women, and Green gave a statement in which she acknowledged her involvement in the crime.[10]

On February 3, 1988, a grand jury returned an indictment in which Green was charged with three counts: "(1) Aggravated murder, for the purposeful killing of Willis, . . . with the specification that Green committed the murder as the principal offender while she was also participating in an aggravated robbery; (2) aggravated robbery, for possessing a deadly weapon while she was committing a theft offense; and (3) felonious assault for an unrelated event that occurred in 1986."[11] The last charge was severed from the other two charges and ultimately dismissed.[12]

After entering a plea of not guilty, Green moved for and obtained the appointment of psychologists and other supporting experts to assist in the preparation of her defense. On June 27, 1988, her trial before a three-judge panel commenced, and three days later she was found guilty of both aggravated murder and aggravated robbery. On July 7, 1988, the penalty phase of her trial began, and the panel concluded, with respect to the aggravated murder, that the aggravating factors outweighed the mitigating factors and that the death penalty was the appropriate sentence. With respect to the aggravated robbery, Green was sentenced to ten to twenty-five years.[13]

Green appealed her conviction and sentence to the First Appellate District of Ohio.[14] She presented four assignments of error: that she was denied her right to confront witnesses against her when the trial court restricted cross-examination of Coulter, that she was denied effective assistance of counsel, that the death penalty was inappropriate for her case, and that the trial court erred in overruling her motion challenging the Ohio death penalty statutes.[15] The appellate court overruled all four assignments of error. It further ruled that the aggravating circumstances of Willis's homicide outweighed the mitigating factors presented and that the sentence of death was appropriate.[16]

Along with Rosalie Grant and Debra Brown, Green saw her death sentence vacated when Governor Richard Celeste commuted the sentences of eight prisoners in 1991.[17] Despite challenges to those commutations,[18] Green ultimately received a life sentence without the possibility of parole.[19] Before the court of appeals confirmed the governor's decision, the Supreme Court of Ohio had affirmed Green's conviction and sentence.[20] In a concurring opinion, Justice Craig Wright wrote that Green's coldly formulated plan far outweighed the evidence of low intellect, advanced chemical dependency, and limited emotional development.[21] In a dissenting opinion,

Justice Paul Pfeifer wrote, with regard to the difference between Coulter's and Green's sentences, that prosecutors should avoid situations in which a plea bargain will result in the death penalty for one defendant as opposed to a greatly reduced charge for another principal in the same crime, thereby allowing the prosecutor determine who was to live and who was to die.[22] Green's petition to the U.S. Supreme Court for a writ of certiorari was also denied.[23]

In an interview in 1989, Green claimed she was innocent, stating, "I am not capable of stabbing someone 100 times. A person like that needs to be in a mental hospital. Do I look like I need to be in a hospital?" Discussing her time in prison, she predicted, "In due time, I will be a much more bitter person. I haven't spent a long time in here, but the short time has been madness. I don't know what I'll be five years later, but I don't think I will be my same self."[24]

There are a few factors that turn against Green. The victim was seventy at the time of his death, and he was stabbed over a hundred times. The motive for robbing the victim was to gain money to purchase cocaine.[25] Particularly damaging to Green and addressed in a dissenting opinion from the Ohio Supreme Court was the use of a plea bargain that worked against Green and in favor of Coulter.[26] Like Debra Brown, Green, who could be classified as mentally retarded,[27] probably would not receive the same sentence today if her mental retardation were considered as a factor in determining her sentence.[28] At the time of trial, Green's lack of emotional development and troubled childhood were not significant enough to give her a sentence less than death.

EIGHTEEN

Beatrice Lampkin

Sentenced in 1989, Commuted in 1991

BEATRICE LAMPKIN was forty-seven years old at the time of her crime, the hiring in 1988 of a hit man to kill her husband.[1] Lampkin and her husband had been married for nearly twenty-five years, during which time he was physically and sexually abusive to her. Lampkin described the abusive relationship to a psychologist who testified in the sentencing phase of her trial. The psychologist spoke of a terrifying pattern of abuse that included regular incidents of sexual torture. Testimony showed that Mr. Lampkin also threatened the couple's children, and Lampkin described one occasion in which he placed a noose around their son's neck and threatened to hang him. The defense asserted that Lampkin suffered from battered woman syndrome and hired the killer because of the terror she faced at home.[2] According to a public defender familiar with the case, the circumstances leading up to the murder-for-hire decision were so horrible, so degrading, and so alien to the way she had been brought up that it changed her ability to cope.[3]

In late 1987, Lampkin asked her daughter's boyfriend if he knew of someone who would kill her husband for $10,000. Lampkin proposed several methods for carrying out the murder at a time when no one in the family would be present. Proposals were discussed for several months, but the boyfriend eventually refused to commit the murder. Lampkin then asked another boyfriend of her daughter's if he knew of someone who would kill her husband. Through this second boyfriend, Lampkin hired the hit man, agreeing to pay him $5,000. Lampkin then drove her daughter and the hit man to the place where they purchased the pistol that was used to kill Mr. Lampkin. Around 5:30 A.M. on November 4, 1988, the hit man, who had been waiting outside the Lampkin residence, shot Mr. Lampkin in the forehead as he was taking out the garbage.[4] The hit man then rode off on a bicycle for about three-quarters of a mile and met up with Lampkin, her daughter, and her daughter's boyfriend. The hit man abandoned the bicycle and got into Lampkin's car.[5] Mr. Lampkin was discovered by the couple's son and his girlfriend as they came home from working the late shift. After two months of investigation, Lampkin confessed and was charged with the aggravated murder for hire of her husband.[6]

The grand jury returned an indictment against Lampkin, charging her with the aggravated murder of her spouse, including a death-penalty specification alleging that the aggravated murder was committed for hire and a firearm specification.[7] A three-judge panel found Lampkin guilty of aggravated murder and both specifications and sentenced her to death.[8] The gunman in the case received only a life sentence.[9]

Lampkin appealed her sentence and conviction and presented five assignments of error. The alleged errors were failure to give proper weight to the mitigating factors, failure to specify which aggravating circumstances and mitigating factors were considered and why the aggravating factors were deemed to outweigh the mitigating factors, failure to prove aggravating circumstances beyond a reasonable doubt, violation of the U.S. and Ohio constitutions through use of the Ohio death penalty statutes, and a sentence excessive and disproportionate. The appellate court considered the assignments of error and concluded that they did not have merit. It affirmed Lampkin's conviction, including the death sentence imposed, on October 3, 1990.[10]

Under Governor Richard Celeste's commutations in 1991, Lampkin received a life sentence with the possibility of parole.[11] When asked how Lampkin felt about the commutation, a public defender familiar with Lampkin's case stated, "I guess she feels grateful for having her life spared. But the truth is, her life hasn't been all that hot anyway."[12] Lampkin first became eligible for parole in 2002.[13] She was denied parole and will be eligible again in 2010.[14]

Lampkin did not herself kill the victim but hired a hit man.[15] What is most interesting is that this is the first mention of battered woman syndrome in the Ohio death penalty cases. Lampkin's decision to hire someone to kill her husband was probably based upon the severe abuse by her husband of her and the couple's children.[16] Lampkin's daughter probably assisted her because of either abuse she herself encountered or abuse she watched her mother encounter at the hands of her father.[17] Given the obvious premeditation involved in carrying out the murder,[18] Lampkin's use of the battered woman syndrome as a special form of self-defense would have been limited. Self-defense typically requires that the person was being attacked at that moment and had no alternative but to use deadly force in her defense.[19] Despite the premeditation involved, however, the specific instances of documented abuse evoke sympathy for Lampkin.

NINETEEN

Donna Roberts

Sentenced in 2003, Now on Death Row

DONNA ROBERTS and her husband, Robert Fingerhut, both white, had a common-law marriage with no children.[1] The couple was in the process of separating,[2] but they were still living together at the time of the commission of the crime. They had resided in Youngstown for approximately two and one-half years with no previous problems.[3] At the time, Fingerhut and Roberts were managing several Greyhound Bus stations.[4]

On December 11, 2001, a Trumbull County dispatcher received a 911 call from Roberts at 12:25 A.M. Dispatchers could not get information from Roberts because she was hysterical, so they dispatched both an ambulance and police officers to the scene.[5] Upon arrival, officers found Fingerhut lying near the garage, dead from three .38-caliber gunshot wounds, one of which was to the back of his head.[6] The only thing missing from the residence was the couple's car. Nothing was disturbed.[7] The police found no weapons,[8] and there were no signs of forced entry.[9] Because of the presence of defensive wounds, the forensic pathologist found that Fingerhut had struggled with his attacker.[10]

Roberts did own a handgun matching the murder weapon's caliber, but the weapon had been reported missing in November 2001.[11] The missing handgun had resulted in charges against Santiago Mason, which were later dismissed at the behest of the prosecutor because it was believed that Roberts falsified the report to cover her own tracks.[12]

The couple's missing silver Chrysler, which was covered in blood, was found the next day by Howland Township Police on Pershing Street in Youngstown.[13] Police arrested Nathaniel Jackson, a black twenty-nine-year-old Youngstown resident.[14] Jackson had just been released from Loraine Correctional Institution earlier that month[15] after serving his sentence for two counts of receiving stolen property.[16] Police with bullhorns were able to coax Jackson to surrender.[17]

A special grand jury convened the next day and issued indictments for both Roberts and Jackson.[18] Both were indicted on December 28, 2001,[19] for capital murder, one count of aggravated burglary with a firearms specification, and one count of aggravated robbery with a firearms specification.[20] Roberts and Jackson pleaded not guilty to all charges.[21]

Roberts was fifty-seven years old at the time of the commission of her crime.[22] There was speculation that Roberts murdered her husband for a new Cadillac and a $325,000 life insurance policy. Information later surfaced that Roberts and Jackson had been lovers for two years prior to the commission of their crimes. Police found 145 handwritten letters from Jackson in Roberts's trunk and 143 handwritten letters from Jackson in Roberts's bedroom.[23] The letters recounted the events of Jackson and Roberts's two-year love affair[24] and detailed a plot to commit murder.[25]

While in custody, Jackson gave a videotaped statement in which he recounted the events of December 11, 2001. Jackson told officers that he and Fingerhut had been arguing when Fingerhut pulled a gun. The two began to wrestle, and the gun discharged twice.[26] At that time, Fingerhut was still breathing,[27] and Jackson fled the scene in Fingerhut's car with Roberts's cell phone. Jackson continually denied Roberts's involvement in Fingerhut's murder.[28]

Jackson further denied planning anything with Roberts. He did admit to calling Roberts after the murder and meeting her at a local hotel, where she bandaged his finger.[29] Roberts also gave a videotaped statement, but counsel in the case agreed not to use her statements because Roberts's constitutional rights were violated when officers continued interrogating her incommunicado after she said she did not want to answer any more questions.[30]

Roberts and Jackson were tried separately. Jackson's jury trial began in October 2002. Jackson maintained that he was lured to Fingerhut's home with the promise of employment. Once Fingerhut and Jackson arrived at the home, Fingerhut began fighting with Jackson over the recently discovered affair. Jackson's counsel argued he was merely acting in self-defense by protecting himself from a jealous husband.[31]

Jurors began deciding Jackson's fate in November of 2002.[32] After three days of deliberation, the eleven-woman and one-man jury convicted Jackson on all counts. Jackson sat expressionless as the jury verdict was read out loud.[33] The penalty phase immediately ensued. Defense counsel put on mitigating evidence supporting a violent traumatic childhood,[34] a low IQ, and an ability to adapt to prison life. The prosecution countered with the numerous handwritten letters by both Jackson and Roberts.[35] Jackson apologized for his actions and begged for his life and the opportunity to watch his daughter grow up.[36] To counter the aggravating circumstances, defense counsel argued that the jurors should consider the disproportionate number of African Americans on death row.[37] Despite all the mitigating evidence, on November 16, 2002, the jury recommended Jackson be sentenced to death.[38]

Roberts's trial began in early April of 2003, and jury selection carried over into May.[39] Pretrial publicity presented special issues in seating a jury because her trial ran subsequent to Jackson's.[40] Eventually, a jury was seated[41] and opening statements were presented. In a stunning move, Roberts gave her own opening statement. Roberts told the jurors, "I'm not guilty and you'll know that when this case is over." Roberts sobbed with her head in her hand while prosecutors read the correspondence between her and Jackson and portrayed her as a greedy soon-to-be-ex-wife.[42] Defense counsel declined to present a single witness and failed to present a closing statement. In summation, defense counsel asked that the instructions be read to the jurors.[43] Roberts's trial lasted approximately two weeks.

Jurors deliberated for a little over an hour before returning with the guilty verdict.[44] Roberts was sentenced to death on June 21, 2003.[45]

Roberts refused to allow her defense counsel to present any witnesses during the penalty phase. Roberts went on a tirade about the criminal justice system's racial inequalities, underqualified public defenders, overzealous prosecutors, lack of impartial juries, and lying witnesses. Once sentenced, Roberts stated, "I got what I wanted." She claimed to have wanted equality in the decisions that sentenced both her and Jackson, an African American male, to death.[46] Roberts welcomed the sentence with a smile[47] as she became the first woman sentenced to death in Ohio since 1991.[48]

As of late 2005, Roberts's case was pending on appeal before the Supreme Court of Ohio.[49] On August 13, 2003, less than two months after her death sentence was imposed, Roberts filed a notice of appeal in the Supreme Court of Ohio. Because the Office of the Ohio Public Defender was representing Roberts's codefendant, Jackson, in his appeal, that office had to withdraw from representing Roberts in her appeal due to conflict of interest. Private attorneys in Cleveland were appointed to represent Roberts on appeal, and they filed their primary brief in her case on July 19, 2004.[50] That brief raised many questions as to Roberts's conviction and death sentence, including major challenges to the failure to present any mitigating evidence at the penalty stage of her trial:

(1) A waiver of the presentation of mitigation evidence in the penalty phase of trial is not valid unless the defendant is informed that the waiver will result in the death sentence. Such waiver is also invalid if the defendant intends to present any mitigation in any form.[51]

(2) A capital defendant's right to allocution before being sentenced is mandatory. Where the sentencing court neglects this right, the subsequent sentence is void or voidable.[52]

(3) The failure to properly advise and ensure that a capital defendant understands the ramifications of a waiver of evidence in the penalty phase constitutes ineffective assistance of counsel.[53]

The first and third issues argue that Roberts should have been more adequately informed, both by the trial judge and by her trial lawyer, of the impact of her refusal to allow any mitigating evidence to be introduced at her penalty trial. Her decision almost guaranteed that she would be sentenced to death, a sentence that Roberts appeared pleased to receive: "She got what I wanted."[54] Of course, Roberts's lawyers are arguing on appeal that Roberts might have made a different decision had she been properly informed. The other part of this claim, that Roberts was denied her right to allocution, refers to the denial of Roberts's right to speak about her sentence prior to deciding to sentence her to death. Presumably, a statement by Roberts might have persuaded the trial judge not to sentence her to death.

This appellate brief raises several other issues as well, including arguments that some of the jurors were biased in favor of the death penalty[55] and that the pretrial publicity was so pervasive that the court should have granted a change of venue so that the case could have been tried somewhere other than in Youngstown.[56] In a final sweeping argument, this brief asserts that the death penalty is unconstitutional as presently administered in Ohio,[57] among other reasons because it discriminates based on the race of the offender.[58] Perhaps for obvious reasons, the argument as to discrimination stops at race bias and does not allege gender bias.

Responding to Roberts's brief before the Ohio Supreme Court, the prosecution filed a response brief on November 1, 2004. As is standard procedure in such cases, the prosecution's brief simply recapitulates the arguments in Roberts's brief and responds to them one by one. Particularly telling may be the prosecution's response to Roberts's assertion of delayed opportunity for allocution: "A capital defendant suffers no prejudice when she is afforded the right of allocution after the sentence is announced from the bench, but before the sentencing hearing is adjourned, when the defendant has already requested a death sentence, thanks the judge for imposing a death sentence, and has waived the right to present any mitigating evidence."[59] Oral arguments in the case are scheduled for early 2006, and a decision by the Supreme Court of Ohio sometime after that.

At the time of her sentencing, Roberts became the only woman on Ohio's death row.[60] Several factors in Roberts's case probably justified, in the jurors' minds, the sentence of death. The letters exchanged between Roberts and Jackson detailed the plot to kill Fingerhut.[61] Plans were made to kill Fingerhut even though he and Roberts were in the process of separating.[62] There was no indication that Roberts suffered any abuse at the hands of Fingerhut, and the couple had no children who would continue to bind them in separation. Fingerhut sustained one bullet wound to the back of his head.[63] This suggests extreme hatred by the shooter.

Events and facts apart from the murder itself were also potentially damaging to Roberts. The jury may have seen Roberts as arrogant when she delivered her own opening statement.[64] Her tirade against the criminal justice system was probably ill-advised.[65] Because Jackson is black,[66] Roberts's affair with him could well have been offensive to the jury. There is also a significant age difference between the two: Jackson, who had just been released from prison, was twenty-nine and Roberts fifty-seven at the time of the crime.[67] Lastly, there was a monetary motive.[68]

TWENTY

Nicole Ann Diar

Sentenced in 2005, Now on Death Row

ON NOVEMBER 2, 2005, thirty-year-old Nicole Ann Diar was sentenced to death in Elyria, Ohio.[1] Diar joined Donna Roberts on death row, doubling the number of women under sentences of death in Ohio.[2] Her appeals are just beginning in what promises to be a very long and drawn-out process.[3] In many ways, Diar's death sentence may be one of the most troubling in Ohio's history.

Diar's death sentence was based upon her conviction for murdering her four-year-old son, Jacob Diar, and burning his body nearly beyond recognition on August 27, 2003.[4] The first media reports characterized Diar as a tragic victim, a "good mother" who was "hysterical" at the scene of the fire. The immediate sympathy toward Diar came largely because she had suffered horrible burns herself in 1979, when she was only four years old, the same age at which her son was consumed by fire.[5] The severe burns to her arms, neck, and face resulted when her then two-year-old brother was playing with a cigarette lighter and accidentally set Diar's nightgown on fire.[6] During the next few years, Diar endured forty surgeries to repair the damage and to allow her to move her head and neck and use a disfigured thumb.[7] The rest of her childhood was marked by predictable teasing and mocking from classmates. A psychologist who interviewed Diar when she was still a child provided a dark prognosis: "I think her adolescence will be prolonged, tormented and distorted, and I believe that her existence will be significantly less happy, more troubled and leave her vulnerable for psychiatric illness; very largely depression." In 1982, the Diar family sued the manufacturers of her flammable nightgown and received a substantial judgment payable to Diar in installments until she is fifty-nine years old.[8]

More than twenty years later, when Diar was twenty-eight, her only child was murdered.[9] This was the child that Diar didn't think she could have due to her own burn injuries; she called Jacob her "miracle baby."[10] At first, Jacob's father, Robert Serrano, did not believe Jacob was his son, but ultimately both the father and the paternal grandparents came to accept and love the child.[11] One of several bizarre elements of the Diar case is that the victim's two grandmothers, Marilyn Diar (maternal) and Muneca Figueroa (paternal), took opposite sides as to Diar's guilt. Deputies would in fact need to break them up after a shouting match in court.[12]

The fire in Diar's modest rental home in Lorain, Ohio, began at about 9:00 A.M. on Wednesday, August 27, 2003.[13] Firefighters believed at the time that the fire had started in Jacob's upstairs bedroom, but it was not until nearly six weeks later that the fire was ruled an arson by the state fire marshal's office. This arson ruling was based upon the county coroner's decision that Jacob had been the victim of "homicidal violence of an undetermined nature"[14] and on the fact that firefighters found traces of gasoline in Jacob's room.[15] At trial, the coroner testified that Jacob had died before the fire occurred, as "the mouth and nostrils were not inflamed with debris and soot from the fire."[16] Prosecutors built upon the coroner's imprecise finding of homicide by undetermined violence and argued to the jury that Diar killed Jacob by suffocation or drowning and then started the fire to destroy the evidence.[17]

Although the findings of criminal homicide and arson were made in October of 2003, it was not until April 30, 2004, that Diar was indicted by a grand jury for capital murder, arson, and related crimes.[18] Diar had already hired a local criminal defense attorney and she turned herself in at the county jail the same day she was indicted.[19] Immediately after the indictment was filed, the county prosecutors made several emotional statements about the case to the press, which were followed by reactions from Diar's attorney.[20] Bizarrely, three weeks later the prosecutors asked the judge to issue a gag order in the case, prohibiting witnesses, attorneys, and court personnel from publicly discussing or commenting on the case.[21] On June 9, 2004, the judge refused to issue the gag order.[22]

Nearly seventeen months passed between Diar's indictment and the beginning of her jury trial, a period filled with many motions and countermotions looking forward to the trial.[23] Diar had posted bail on June 22, 2004, less than two months after she had been indicted and had entered jail.[24] Her trial began in the county seat town of Elyria, Ohio, on September 26, 2005.[25] It took five court days to impanel the jury of eight women and four men, and, after delays for the court to consider various motions, the jury began to hear the evidence on Monday, October 3, 2005.[26] Court TV was there from the beginning, promising to record the proceedings from gavel to gavel and broadcast them on delay.[27]

The prosecution's basic argument was that Diar first asphyxiated Jacob and then created an intense fire that destroyed almost all evidence of how he died.[28] The fire was so intense that parts of Jacob's body, according to the coroner who examined it, had literally disappeared: "The bones of the forearms were incinerated. They were absolutely incinerated into nothingness." Investigators found traces of gasoline on the floor and furniture in the bedroom in which Jacob was found, as well as in the living room and dining room, and concluded that the gasoline had been used to start and to accelerate the fire.[29] However, the state had no direct evidence of exactly how Jacob died, and it certainly had no direct evidence that Diar killed Jacob.[30] As for the gasoline, the state could not find that Diar had gasoline on her clothes or her body, or that she even had a gasoline can in the house.[31] However, the state did pound home evidence that Diar appeared to be more interested in partying than in being a good mother, and that she even went out drinking and dancing at a bar on the night of Jacob's funeral.[32] Court TV summarized the state's case as follows: "Prosecutors presented an eight-day, thirty-four-witness case that was light on physical evidence but heavy on Diar's poor parenting skills and penchant for leaving Jacob with teenage babysitters while she went out at night."[33]

Diar's lawyer admitted that she "wasn't the best mother" but focused on the state's lack of evidence that Diar killed her child or that Diar started the fire.[34] The defense also raised the possibility that someone else committed the crimes, perhaps an unknown intruder who had a grudge against Diar.[35] Questions were raised about the origin of the fire, and the original fire investigator's report was shown to contain several admitted errors.[36] Diar's lawyers also presented evidence, including testimony by Diar's mother and pastor, that she deeply mourned the death of her son.[37] Such evidence usually is reserved for the mitigation stage of the death sentencing hearing, but it apparently was used here to refute the state's claim that Diar was an uncaring mother.[38]

On Monday morning, October 17, 2005, the attorneys made their closing arguments, and the jury retired to begin its deliberations.[39] Despite the lack of direct evidence, the jury took less than four hours to find Diar guilty of the murder, arson, and related crimes.[40] Later, the jury forewoman seemed to have no doubts about the jury's decision: "It was a very conscientious group who took their responsibility very seriously. We found her guilty on 10 counts. The evidence supported that in every instance. There was no pleasure in having to rule in that fashion, but it was the evidence and it was the truth."[41]

The sentencing hearing began and ended on November 1, 2005.[42] Following opening statements, the state argued that the aggravating circumstance—the fact that Jacob was younger than thirteen—was ample basis for imposing the death penalty. The state did not claim an additional aggravating circumstance of the murder being committed during the felony of arson, presumably since there was no evidence that these two crimes were committed at essentially the same time. The defense presentation at the sentencing hearing was extremely brief, consisting of only two witnesses. The first, a forensic psychologist, testified that Diar suffers from a personality disorder that prevents her from separating reality from illusion, stating, "She was handicapped from the time she was scarred."[43] Diar's mother was her second and final witness, testifying briefly and pleading for her daughter's life: "We love our daughter very, very much. I ask that you spare her life."[44]

The jury retired for its final deliberations that same afternoon and then returned to continue deliberations at 9:00 A.M. the next day (November 2).[45] Shortly after lunch, the jury returned a verdict recommending death.[46]

Diar was asked if she had any last words before the judge imposed the court's sentence, and she continued her claim of innocence. "I didn't kill my son. I couldn't show remorse for something I didn't do. I am really sorry that people feel that way." Seconds later, the trial court judge accepted the jury's recommendation and sentenced Diar to death. Following sentencing, Jacob's maternal grandmother (Diar's mother) got into a shouting match with Jacob's paternal grandmother, requiring deputies to break up the fight and escort the family out of the courthouse.[47] Apparently some of the jurors approached the trial judge after the verdicts and asked, "Did we do the right thing?" The judge responded that "I probably would have done the same thing."[48]

As of this writing, only a few weeks have passed since Nicole Diar was sentenced to death. Diar continues to enjoy the unwavering support of her parents and her lawyers.[49] Her trial lawyers are preparing an appeal and are seeking to include experienced death penalty appellate lawyers on their team.[50] Meanwhile, the community of Lorain, Ohio, is trying to put this tragic event behind it, including by renovating the house where Jacob died, with hopes to sell it in early 2006.[51] Diar has moved to death row, and her case will continue.[52]

PART FIVE

Comparing and Contrasting Cases

TWENTY-ONE

Executed Women, 1803–2005

BECAUSE ONLY four women have ever been executed in Ohio, a meaningful comparison of their cases is difficult. The extent of the pool of potentially capital cases represented by these four actual executions is unknown. Probably several times this many women were sentenced to death but never executed prior to the 1970s, and presumably hundreds, perhaps thousands, of women committed capital crimes but were never sentenced to death. While it is tempting to assume that these four executions were imposed in the four very worst cases, there is no empirical context for such a conclusion.

The execution cases may be most easily compared in sets of two. Hester Foster and Betty Butler are the first set: black adult women[1] convicted of violently killing other adult women[2] who were not strangers to them.[3] Foster and Butler were the only offenders among these four executed women who killed female victims. Foster killed a white woman,[4] and Butler killed a black woman.[5] Both were shockingly violent crimes. Foster beat her victim to death with a shovel,[6] while Butler beat, strangled, and drowned her victim.[7] Foster had an accomplice who was described as "another colored woman,"[8] but Butler committed her murder alone.[9]

Not enough is known about Foster's crime to speculate about possible defenses or mitigation. In any event, one can assume that a black prisoner who committed murder in the 1840s did not have access to top-flight counsel to raise any defenses or mitigation. In that time period, one also can assume that a black-on-white homicide was particularly frowned upon by those trying the case and making the death penalty decision.

There is a more extensive record regarding Butler's case, and it does raise several possibilities. Butler's enraged beating of her victim as a reaction to allegedly being the victim's sex slave[10] at least should have been a strong mitigating factor[11] and might well have reduced the crime from murder to voluntary manslaughter.[12] This reduction in crime category from murder to manslaughter would have avoided the death penalty for Butler.[13] However, Butler's crime was committed in a public setting with several witnesses,[14] so she hardly could have claimed that she didn't do it. Also going against Butler, at least off the record, was the fact that she was a black woman involved in a sexual relationship with another black woman, whether voluntarily or not.[15] In 1950s Ohio, this would have relegated the value of her life to the bottom of the stack.

The second pair of women's cases is that of Anna Marie Hahn and Dovie Blanche Dean, the similarities of which were noted even by Dean's prosecuting attorney.[16] Both women killed elderly white males by administering arsenic. The nature of the homicides indicates that proof of premeditation would have been fairly easy, but their crimes did not involve any physical violence,[17] certainly as compared to the violent beatings by Foster and Butler. In both the Hahn and Dean cases, the defendants' sons were involved as witnesses and could possibly have been accomplices, although that point was never proven in either case.[18] Both women confessed to their crimes, but Dean repudiated her confession,[19] and Hahn confessed only through letters published after her execution.[20] The women's motives may have been profit,[21] but there is considerable doubt of that in the Dean case.[22]

The attitudes of Hahn and Dean at trial reportedly were similar. Hahn was described as stoic, poker-faced, and passive, with no display of resentment or shock. She was cool and poised, paying no attention to the large crowd.[23] Dean appeared extremely confident and was at ease on the witness stand.[24] Her manner conveyed the impression that her mind was far from the courtroom.[25] With regard to differences between Hahn and Dean, both women knew their victims, but Hahn's victims were friends or acquaintances,[26] and Dean's victim was her husband.[27] Also, even though Hahn was tried for the murder of just one man, she was accused of killing four or more men,[28] while Dean had only one victim.[29]

Putting these cases into their respective time periods, they appear to be completely isolated events. Foster was executed in 1844 and apparently was the only woman executed during Ohio's first one and one-third centuries. Hahn, tried in 1937 and executed in 1938, was characterized in the press as a "blonde German woman" and in fact had been born in Germany, immigrating to the United States only a few years prior to her string of homicides.[30] By the late 1930s, anti-German feeling was growing increasingly widespread. Moreover, the 1930s were a peak decade for executions of both men and women in Ohio and nationally,[31] so it would not be surprising to find one of the rare executions of an Ohio woman in this decade.

In striking contrast, it is quite surprising to find that two of the four executions of Ohio women occurred in 1954. The 1950s were a decade of rapidly declining executions—certainly of men and, to a lesser degree, of women—both in Ohio and nationally. For example, Foster's 1844 execution accounted for 1 (0.8 percent) of Ohio's 126 executions prior to 1890; Hahn's 1938 execution accounted for 1 (1.2 percent) of Ohio's 82 executions in the 1930s; and Dean's and Butler's 1954 executions were 2 (6.3 percent) of Ohio's 32 executions in the 1950s.[32] Dean, a fifty-four-year-old white farm woman,[33] and Butler, a twenty-four-year-old black woman living in Cincinnati,[34] could not have been more different individuals. Nor were their crimes in any way alike. Dean poisoned her elderly husband,[35] whereas Butler beat, strangled, and drowned her black lesbian lover.[36] Nonetheless, these two women were the last to be executed in Ohio, dying within less than five months of each other.[37]

The cases of the four women executed in Ohio have very few similarities, beyond all being homicides committed by women. The Hahn case might be characterized as uniquely serious since it involved a serial killer, but the other three do not seem to stand out as particularly heinous in comparison with other homicides committed during the past two centuries in Ohio. They occurred over a 110-year period (1844–1954), but, again with the exception of Hahn, they do not appear to correlate with political movements or events that might help to explain them. A half century has now passed since Ohio's last execution of a woman, and the mystery continues. Perhaps, until more is known, one can characterize the execution of women in Ohio only as sporadic and lacking any apparent rational basis.

TWENTY-TWO

Death-Sentenced Women, 1973–2005

THE PREVIOUS chapter's analysis of the cases of women executed in Ohio since 1803 was limited by the lack of reliable data on the number of women sentenced to death in the state but not executed. The analysis here of cases of women sentenced to death in Ohio since 1973 (the beginning of the current death penalty era nationally) is limited by the fact that none of them has been executed. Furthermore, given the significantly different legal environment of the death penalty in the current era as compared to previous eras (pre-1973), one cannot make meaningful comparisons between the women sentenced to death since 1973 and the women actually executed prior to 1973.

The appropriate comparisons, then, are those between and among the eleven women sentenced to death in Ohio in the current era. Six of the eleven were black women, and five of those six were in their early twenties when their crimes were committed. The odd case here is that of Lampkin, a black woman forty-seven years old at the time she hired a hit man to kill her husband.[1] Roberts was a fifty-seven-year-old white woman, but her codefendant and lover was a much younger black man, a fact that played a key role in the case.[2] This leaves only four of the eleven cases (Diar, Osborne, Wernert, and Young) in which a white woman was sentenced to death for a murder which did not involve any black codefendants. Two of these white women (Osborne and Wernert) killed victims who were white women.[3] Two other white women sentenced to death killed white men: Young, a bartender,[4] and Roberts, her husband.[5] These few cases are not sufficient for sophisticated quantitative analysis, but it does appear that race of offender and race of victim are factors in sentencing women to death in the current era.

At least six of these eleven women had significant issues of mental competency at the times of their crimes. Two (Brown and Green) apparently were mentally retarded[6] and presumably would not be sentenced to death currently under the holding of *Atkins v. Virginia.*[7] Lockett was a recovering heroin addict,[8] and Young presumably was intoxicated with alcohol at the time of her crime.[9] Grant apparently suffered from postpartum depression, and Brown and Lampkin arguably suffered from battered woman syndrome.[10] At a minimum, then, three of these women (Brown, Green, and Lampkin) would be extremely unlikely to receive a death sentence today.

These eleven women's death sentences came from judges and juries scattered around Ohio, from Cincinnati to Toledo to Cleveland, but all came from urban or suburban communities. Nine of the sentences were imposed between 1975 and 1989, a pace of nearly one sentence per year except for the five-year lull (1978–82) during the change in Ohio's death penalty statute.[11] The tenth sentence, in 2003, followed a fourteen-year period (1989–2003) in which no women were sentenced to death in Ohio. This lull may have been caused in part by Governor Celeste's extraordinary grant of clemency to all of the women on death row in January 1991,[12] but more than twelve years passed before another woman was sentenced to death following that clemency order.

A final observation about these eleven death sentences is that seven of them were imposed upon women who did not kill the victim(s) themselves. Case opinions in death penalty law (e.g., *Tison v. Arizona, Enmund v. Florida*) have established that such capital offenders nonetheless must have participated in the felonies in a major way and must have manifested a reckless indifference to human life if they are to be sentenced to death.[13] Only three (Brown, Lampkin, and Roberts) of these seven women were sentenced after these cases were handed down, and the facts of their cases may well satisfy this *Tison-Enmund* test. The other four (Lockett, Osborne, Wernert, and Smith) preceded the test, but they do match the pattern of death-sentenced women who usually did not kill the victim(s) themselves. This pattern is reflected nationally as well: the typical woman on death row is associated in the crime with someone else (almost always a man) who does the actual killing.[14]

Conclusion

ONLY FOUR women have been executed in Ohio's more than two centuries of statehood, and only eleven have been sentenced to death in the thirty-plus years of the current death penalty era. Thousands of women have committed murder in Ohio since 1803 and over a hundred have done so since 1973. Why were these cases singled out for this rare honor? Is there something about the Ohio capital punishment system that works against the death penalty for women generally, but nonetheless allowed these particular death sentences and executions to proceed?

Women are underrepresented nationally on death rows and in execution chambers, and Ohio is certainly no exception. It seems apparent that a subtle and unspoken bias based upon the sex of the offender is operating here.[1] If the measure is actual executions, Ohio has executed 481 persons, only 4 (less than 1 percent) of whom have been females. Nationally, executions of women or girls have constituted just under 3 percent of all executions, suggesting that Ohio's sex bias may be even stronger than it has been nationally.[2] An analysis of Ohio's death penalty laws from before statehood to the current era, however, reveals no obvious intent to formalize a bias against imposing the death penalty upon female offenders.[3] Ohio's bias against this practice appears to be implied and cultural rather than express and legal.

The four female offenders executed in Ohio were women well into adulthood. Ohio has never executed a girl who was under the age of eighteen at the time of her crime.[4] A beginning assumption about Ohio's four executed women might be that they were in a special category with common characteristics. Even a brief review, however, reveals striking differences among these four cases. The first was a middle-aged black woman who violently killed a fellow white prisoner in the 1840s.[5] The second was a white German immigrant who quietly poisoned the elderly white men for whom she cared in the 1930s.[6] The last two Ohio women were executed less than five months apart in 1954. One was a grandmotherly white farm wife who poisoned her elderly husband,[7] and the other was a young urban black woman who violently fought and killed a black woman who had sexually enslaved her.[8] Beyond the disparate facts of these cases, just staring at their photographs is striking evidence that four more different women or settings would be hard to imagine.

Has this Ohio practice changed during the current death penalty era? The eleven women sentenced to death in Ohio during the past thirty years seem less dissimilar, but finding clear themes is difficult. As discussed in chapter 22, these women's crimes ranged from murder committed in the course of armed robbery to killing family members, and the women came from several parts of the state and several different backgrounds. As with the four women actually executed in Ohio, it would be difficult to explain why these eleven women were sentenced to death for their crimes while the hundreds of other Ohio women who committed murder were not.

Ohio appears to mirror the national experience in the current death penalty era, except that Ohio may be more reluctant than most states to sentence women to death or to execute them. Current data indicate that exactly one-third (47/144) of the women sentenced to death outside of Ohio are still on death row.[9] However, only two of the eleven women sentenced to death in Ohio are still on death row.[10] Similarly, while just under 1 percent (11/144) of the women sentenced to death outside of Ohio have actually been executed, none of the women sentenced to death in Ohio have been executed.[11] If a death penalty sex bias exists in other death penalty jurisdictions, it appears to be even stronger in Ohio.

Providing proof beyond a reasonable doubt of a bias in death penalty cases in Ohio based upon the sex of the offender is a task left to subsequent efforts. There is considerable evidence of sex bias, but it is more important to document the stories of these fifteen women. Up until now they have largely been condemned, ignored, and forgotten. Our effort certainly cannot change the fact that each of them was condemned (although nine of the eleven most recently condemned are condemned no longer). What we hope we have accomplished is to assure that, although condemned, they will no longer be ignored or forgotten.

Case Summaries for Female Offenders under Death Sentences as of December 31, 2005

Alabama

(last execution of a female by Alabama on 5/10/2002)
(1 female offender now on Alabama's death row)

Blackmon, Patricia

Black; age 29 at crime and now age 36 (DOB: 11/3/1969); murder of black female age 2 (her adopted daughter) in Dothan in May 1999; sentenced on 6/7/2002.

Arizona

(last execution of a female by Arizona on 2/21/1930)
(2 female offenders now on Arizona's death row)

Andriano, Wendi

White; age 30 at crime and now age 35 (DOB: 8/6/1970); murder of white (?) male age 33 (her husband) in Mesa on 10/8/2000; sentenced on 12/22/2004.

Milke, Debra Jean

White; age 25 at crime and now age 41 (DOB: 3/10/1964); murder of white male age 4 (her son) in Maricopa County on 12/2/1989; sentenced on 1/18/1991.

California

(last execution of a female by California on 8/8/1962)
(14 female offenders now on California's death row)

Alfaro, Maria Delrio (Rosie)

Latin; age 18 at crime and now age 34 (DOB: 10/12/1971); burglary, robbery, and murder of Latin girl age 9 in Anaheim on 6/15/1990; sentenced 7/14/1992.

Buenrostro, Dora Luz

Latin; age 34 at crime and now age 45; murder of Latin females ages 4 and 9 and Latin male age 8 (her children) in San Jacinto on 10/25/1994 and 10/27/1994; sentenced on 10/2/1998.

Caro, Socorro

Latin; age 42 at crime and now age 48 (DOB: 3/27/1957); murder of Latin males ages 5, 8, and 11 (her children) in Santa Rosa Valley (Ventura County) on 11/22/1999; sentenced on 4/5/2002.

Carrington, Celeste Simone

Black; age 30 at crimes and now age 44; murders (during burglaries) of Latin male age 34 on 1/26/1992 in San Carlos and of white female age 36 in Palo Alto on 3/11/1992; sentenced on 11/23/1994.

Coffman, Cynthia Lynn

White; age 24 at crime and now age 43 (DOB: 1/19/1962); murder of white female age 20 in San Bernardino County on 11/7/1986; sentenced on 8/31/1989.

Dalton, Kerry Lynn

White; age 28 at crime and now age 45; murder of white female age 23 in Live Oak Springs on 6/26/1988; sentenced on 5/23/1995.

Eubanks, Susan

White; age 33 at crime and now age 42; murder of four white males ages 4, 6, 7, and 14 (her children) in San Marcos (San Diego County) on 10/27/1996; sentenced on 10/13/1999.

Gonzalez, Veronica

Latin; age 26 at crime and now age 36; murder of Latin female age 4 (her niece) in San Diego on 7/21/1995; sentenced on 7/20/1998.

McDermott, Maureen

White; age 37 at crime and now age 58 (DOB: 5/15/1947); murder of white male age 27 in Van Nuys (Los Angeles County) on 4/28/1985; sentenced on 6/8/1990.

Michaud, Michelle Lyn

White; age 38 at crime and now age 44; kidnapping, sexual assault, and murder of white female age 22 in Pleasanton (Alameda County) on 12/2/1997; sentenced on 9/25/2002.

Nieves, Sandi Dawn

White; age 34 at crime and now age 41; murder of four Latin females ages 5, 7, 11, and 12 (her children) in Saugus (north of Los Angeles) on 6/30/1998; sentenced on 10/6/2000.

Rodriguez, Angelina

Latin; age 32 at crime and now age 37; murder of Latin male age 41 (her husband) in Montebello (Los Angeles County) on 9/9/2000; sentenced on 1/12/2004.

Samuels, Mary Ellen

White; age 40 at crimes and now age 56; murder (she hired killer) of white male age 40 (her husband) on 12/8/1988 in Northridge (Los Angeles County) and of white male age 27 (her husband's killer) in Ventura County on 6/27/1989; sentenced on 9/16/1994.

Thompson, Catherine

Black; age 42 at crime and now age 57; murder (she hired killer) of black male (her husband) in Westwood (Los Angeles County) on 6/14/1990; sentenced on 6/10/1993.

Delaware

(last execution of a female by Delaware on 6/7/1935)
(1 female offender on Delaware's death row)

Charbonneau, Linda Lou

White; age 53 at crime and now age 57 (DOB: 2/9/1948); murder of white male age 62 (her ex-husband) near Millsboro (Sussex County) on 9/23/2001 and of white male age 45 (her husband) near Bridgeville (Sussex County) on 10/17/2001; sentenced on 6/4/2004.

Federal

(last execution of a female by the federal government on 12/18/1953)
(1 female offender now on federal death row)

Johnson, Angela Jane

White; age 29 at crime and now age 41; murder of white male age 34, white female age 31, white female age 10, and white female age 6 in Mason City, Iowa, on 7/25/1993, and murder of white male age 32 in Mason City, Iowa, on 11/5/1993; sentenced on 12/20/2005.

Georgia

(last execution of a female by Georgia on 3/5/1945)
(1 female offender now on Georgia's death row)

Brookshire (Gissendaner), Kelly Renee

White, age 28 at crime and now age 37; murder of white male age 30 (her husband) in Gwinnett County on 2/7/1997; sentenced on 11/20/1998.

Idaho

(Idaho has never executed a female offender)
(1 female offender now on Idaho's death row)

Row, Robin Lee

White; age 35 at crime and now age 48 (DOB: 9/12/1957); arson/murder of white male age 34 (her husband), white male age 10 (her son), and white female age 8 (her daughter) in Boise on February 10, 1992; sentenced on 12/16/1993.

Indiana

(Indiana has never executed a female offender)
(1 female offender now on Indiana's death row)

Brown, Debra Denise

Black; age 21 at crime and now age 43 (DOB: 11/11/1962); murder of black female age 7 in Gary on 6/18/1984; sentenced on 6/23/1986; serving life sentence in Ohio but sentenced to death in Indiana.

Kentucky

(last execution of a female by Kentucky on 2/7/1868)
(1 female offender now on Kentucky's death row)

Caudill, Virginia Susan

White; age 37 at crime and now age 45 (DOB: 9/10/1960); robbery and murder of black female age 73 in Lexington on 3/15/1998; sentenced on 3/24/2000.

Louisiana

(last execution of a female by Louisiana on 11/28/1942)
(1 female offender now on Louisiana's death row)

Frank, Antoinette

Black; age 24 at crime and now age 34 (DOB: 4/30/1971); robbery and murder of white male age 25 (police officer), Asian male age 17, and Asian female age 24 in New Orleans on 3/4/1994; sentenced on 9/13/1995.

Mississippi

(last execution of a female by Mississippi on 5/19/1944)
(1 female offender now on Mississippi's death row)

Byrom, Michelle

White; age 43 at crime and now age 49 (DOB: 11/3/1956): murder (she hired killer) of white male age 56 (her husband) in Tishomingo County on 6/4/1999; sentenced on 11/18/2000.

North Carolina

(last execution of a female by North Carolina on 11/2/1984)
(4 female offenders now on North Carolina's death row)

Jennings, Patricia JoAnn [Wells]

White; age 47 at crime and now age 63 (DOB: 8/24/1942); murder of white male age 77 (her husband) in Wilson County on 9/19/1989; sentenced on 11/5/1990.

Moore, Blanche Kiser [Taylor]

White; age 56 at crime and now age 72 (DOB: 2/17/1933); murder of white male age 50 (her boyfriend) in Alamance County on 10/7/1986; sentenced on 11/16/1990.

Parker, Carlette Elizabeth

Black; age 34 at crime and now age 42 (DOB: 6/12/1963); murder of white female age 86 in North Raleigh (Wake County) on 5/12/98; sentenced on 4/1/99.

Walters, Christina S.

American Indian; age 20 at crime and now age 27 (DOB: 7/15/1978); murder of white female age 19 and white female age 25 north of Fayetteville in Cumberland County on 8/17/1998; sentenced on 7/6/2000.

Ohio

(last execution of a female by Ohio on 6/12/1954)
(2 female offenders now on Ohio's death row)

Diar, Nicole Ann

White; age 28 at crime and now age 30 (DOB: 7/21/1975); murder of Latin male age 4 (her son) in Lorain on 8/27/2003; sentenced on 11/2/2005.

Roberts, Donna

White; age 58 at crime and now age 61 (DOB: 5/23/1944); murder of white male (her husband) near Warren (Trumbull County) on 12/11/2001; sentenced on 6/21/2003.

Oklahoma

(last execution of a female by Oklahoma on 12/4/2001)
(1 female offender on Oklahoma's death row)

Andrew, Brenda E.

White; age 37 at crime and now age 42 (DOB: 12/16/1963); murder of white male age 39 (her husband) in Oklahoma City on 11/20/2001; sentenced on 9/22/2004.

Pennsylvania

(last execution of a female by Pennsylvania on 10/14/1946)
(5 female offenders now on Pennsylvania's death row)

Hill, Donetta Marie (Williams)

Black; ages 23 and 24 at crimes and now age 39 (DOB: 9/23/1966); murders of Asian male age 72 in Philadelphia on 6/20/1990 and of black male age 21 in Philadelphia on 3/24/1991; sentenced on 4/9/1992.

King, Carolyn Ann (Ewell; Kline)

Black; age 28 at crime and now age 40 (DOB: 12/9/1965); robbery and murder of white female adult in October 1993 in Lebanon; sentenced on 11/30/1994.

Markman, Beth Ann (Carpenter; Gaylord)

White; age 34 at crime and now age 39 (DOB: 1/6/1966); kidnapping and murder of white (?) female age 18 in Cumberland County on 10/4/2000; sentenced in 2001.

Tharp, Michelle Sue

White; age 29 at crime and now age 36 (DOB: 1/20/1969); murder of white female age 7 (her daughter) in Burgettstown (Washington County) on 4/18/1998; sentenced on 11/14/2000.

Walter (aka Walters), Shondra Dee

Black; age 23 at crime and now age 26 (DOB: 7/16/1979); murder of white male age 83 in Lock Haven (Clinton County) on 3/25/2003; sentenced on 4/19/2005.

Tennessee

(last execution of a female by Tennessee in 1837)
(2 female offenders now on Tennessee's death row)

Owens, Gail (aka Gaile) Kirksey

White; age 32 at crime and now age 53 (DOB: 9/22/1952); murder (she hired killer) of white male (her husband) in Shelby County on 2/17/1985; sentenced on 1/15/1986.

Pike, Christa Gail

White; age 18 at crime and now age 29 (DOB: 3/10/1976); murder of Latin female age 19 in Knoxville on 1/12/1995; sentenced on 3/29/1996.

Texas

(last execution of a female by Texas on 9/14/2005)
(9 female offenders now on Texas's death row)

Basso, Suzanne Margaret

White; age 44 at crime and now age 51 (DOB: 5/15/1954); murder of white male age 59 (her boyfriend) in Houston on 8/25/1998; sentenced on 9/1/1999.

Berry, Kenisha

Black; age 25 at crime and now age 33 (DOB: 12/26/1972); murder of black male newborn (her son) in Beaumont on 11/29/1998; sentenced on 2/19/2004.

Carty, Linda Anita

Black; age 42 at crime and now age 47 (DOB: 10/5/1958); kidnapping and murder of Latin female age 20 and victim's infant son in Houston on 5/16/2001; sentenced on 2/21/2002.

Henderson, Cathy Lynn

White; age 37 at crime and now age 49 (DOB: 12/27/1956); murder of white male age 3 months (she was babysitter) near Austin (Travis County) on 1/21/1994; sentenced on 5/25/1995.

Holberg, Brittany Marlowe

White; age 23 at crime and now age 32 (DOB: 1/7/1973); murder of white male age 80 in Amarillo on 11/13/1996; sentenced on 3/27/1998.

McCarthy, Kimberly Lagayle

Black; age 36 at crime and now age 44 (DOB: 5/11/1961); murder of white female age 71 in Lancaster (Dallas County) on 7/21/1997; sentenced on 12/?/1998; reversed in 2001; re-sentenced on 11/1/2002.

Richardson, Chelsea Lea

White; age 19 at crime and now age 21 (DOB: 3/26/1984); murder of white male age 46 and white female age 45 in Mansfield (Tarrant County) on 12/11/2003; sentenced on 6/1/2005.

Routier, Darla Lynn

White; age 26 at crime and now age 35 (DOB: 1/4/1970); murder of white male age 5 (her son) in Rowlett (Dallas County) on 6/6/1996; sentenced on 2/4/1997.

Sheppard, Erica Yvonne

Black; age 19 at crime and now age 32 (DOB: 9/1/1973); murder of white (?) female age 43 in Houston on 6/30/1993; sentenced on 3/3/1995.

Virginia

(last execution of a female by Virginia on 8/16/1912)
(1 female offender now on Virginia's death row)

Lewis, Teresa Michelle

White; age 33 at crime and now age 36; murder of white male age 51 (her husband) and white male age 26 (her stepson) in Keeling (Pittsylvania County) on 10/30/2002; sentenced on 6/3/2003.

NOTES

Introduction

1. This is well documented, at least for the past century. See L. Kay Gillespie, *Dancehall Ladies: Executed Women of the 20th Century* (Lanham, Md.: University Press of America, 2000); Kathleen A. O'Shea, *Women and the Death Penalty in the United States, 1900–1998* (Westport, Conn.: Praeger, 1999); and Victor L. Streib, "Gendering the Death Penalty: Countering Sex Bias in a Masculine Sanctuary," *Ohio State Law Journal* 63, no. 1 (2002): 472–74. See also chapter 6. The history of England and Wales is essentially similar, where under 2 percent of executions between 1900 and 1950 were of women. Anette Ballinger, *Dead Woman Walking: Executed Women in England and Wales, 1900–1955* (Aldershot, England: Ashgate, 2000), 1–2, 328. See also Patrick Wilson, *Murderess: A Study of the Women Executed in Britain Since 1843* (London: Michael Joseph, 1971).

2. Notable exceptions to this media disinterest do exist. See, e.g., Sam Howe Verhovek, "Dead Women Waiting: Who's Who on Death Row," *New York Times,* February 8, 1998. A recent investigative report is Rachel King and Judy Bellin, *The Forgotten Population: A Look at Death Row in the United States through the Experiences of Women* (New York: American Civil Liberties Union and American Friends Service Committee, 2004).

3. See, e.g., Sam Howe Verhovek, "As Woman's Execution Nears, Texas Squirms," *New York Times,* January 1, 1998; Verhovek, "Divisive Case of a Killer of Two Ends as Texas Executes Tucker," *New York Times,* February 4, 1998; and Verhovek, "Texas, in First Time in 135 Years, Is Set to Execute Woman," *New York Times,* February 3, 1998. See also Streib, "Gendering the Death Penalty," 451–53.

4. See David A. Kaplan and Nadine Joseph, "'Live, From San Quentin . . . ,'" *Newsweek,* April 1, 1991, 61.

5. Ibid.; "Funerals Held for Gray, Mrs. Snyder," *New York Daily News,* January 14, 1928.

6. A reasoned, reliable, and accurate exception is Wenzell Brown, *Women Who Died in the Chair: The Dramatic True Stories of Six Women Who Committed the Deadliest Sin* (New York: Collier, 1958). Despite its subtitle, Brown's book nonetheless attempts a relatively sober assessment of the larger issues (Brown's last chapter is titled "Was It Worth While?"). Another reasoned work is Bernard O'Donnell,

Should Women Hang? (London: W. H. Allen, 1956). A more sensational example is Tom Kuncl, *Death Row Women* (New York: Pocket Books, 1994), promoted on its cover with the phrases "They killed for money, for love, for kicks. Now, they await the final judgment. . . ." and "The Shocking True Stories of America's Most Vicious Female Killers." Sober assessment by Kuncl is limited to his brief introduction (ix).

7. *Monster* (Media 8 Entertainment and New Market Films, 2003).

8. Nick Broomfield and Joan Churchill, *Aileen: Life and Death of a Serial Killer* (2004), http://www.aileenfilm.com; and Nick Broomfield, *Aileen Wuornos: The Selling of a Serial Killer* (1992), http://www.nickbroomfield.com/aileenwuornos .html. See Nancy Ramsey, "Portraits of a Social Outcast Turned Serial Killer," *New York Times,* December 30, 2003.

9. *I Want To Live* (Figaro Films and United Artists, 1958).

10. On Hollywood's treatment and reception of death penalty stories and the phenomenon of such roles boosting acting careers, see, e.g., John Anderson, "The Movies Seldom Combine Real Life with Death Penalty Situations; Dramatic Tension and Pathos, Not the Justice of State-Sponsored Executions, Are the Stuff of Most Films on the Subject," *Los Angeles Times,* March 17, 2003; Michael Sauter, "Killer Chicks; They Shoot, and Sometimes They Score—On Oscar Night, Look for Actresses in Deadly Roles," *Entertainment Weekly Oscar Guide 2004,* February 6, 2004, 52; Wolfgang Saxon, "Nelson Gidding, 84, Screenwriter of Classics Like 'I Want to Live!'" *New York Times,* May 14, 2004; and Jim Sherlock, "The Green Mile to Movie Stardom," *Herald Sun* (Melbourne, Australia), April 7, 2004. See also Roberta M. Harding, "Celluloid Death: Cinematic Depictions of Capital Punishment," *University of San Francisco Law Review* 30 (Summer 1996): 1167–79.

11. *Last Dance* (Touchstone Pictures and Buena Vista Pictures, 1996). The author provided assorted information to the writer-producer of *Last Dance* early in the writing process and then subsequently to Walt Disney Studios and Touchstone Pictures for use in promoting the film. However, despite (because of?) the author's minor involvement, *Last Dance,* unlike *Monster* or *I Want to Live,* was not well received by the critics. See, e.g., Geoff Brown, "Penn Portrait Shaded with a Heavy Hand," *Times* (London), August 15, 1996; and Janet Maslin, "Death Row Diva: A Raw Sharon Stone," *New York Times,* May 3, 1996.

12. O'Shea, *Women and the Death Penalty,* xix. On the general tendency for women prisoners to be overlooked, see Beverly R. Fletcher, Lynda Dixon Shaver, and Dreama G. Moon, eds., *Women Prisoners: A Forgotten Population* (Westport, Conn.: Praeger, 1993). Two excellent works that seek to reduce this problem are Jane Evelyn Atwood, *Too Much Time: Women in Prison* (Paris: Phaidon, 2000); and Paula C. Johnson, *Inner Lives: Voices of African American Women in Prison* (New York: New York University Press, 2003). See also Ann Jones, *Women Who Kill* (New York: Fawcett Columbine, 1980). The recent investigative report is King and Bellin, *Forgotten Population.* The quote on similar ignorance of such cases in Britain is from Ballinger, *Dead Woman Walking,* 342.

13. See, e.g., O'Shea, *Women and the Death Penalty;* Elizabeth Rapaport, "The Death Penalty and Gender Discrimination," *Law and Society Review* 25, no. 2 (1991): 367–83; and Streib, "Gendering the Death Penalty." Information about women sentenced to death and executed during the current era (1973–present) of the death penalty can be found in the author's quarterly report: Victor L. Streib, "Death Penalty for Female Offenders" (quarterly Web report), http://www.law .onu.edu/faculty/streib/streib.htm.

14. O'Shea, *Women and the Death Penalty,* provides a very helpful sketch of each state's experience with the death penalty for women, but that book's national scope precludes in-depth treatment of each jurisdiction. It also is limited essentially to post-1900 cases (but see 1–15), as is Gillespie, *Dancehall Ladies.* However, executions of women on American soil go back at least to the 1632 execution of Jane Champion in Virginia. See Streib, "Gendering the Death Penalty," 472n175. Ballinger, *Dead Woman Walking,* is a scholarly work with wonderful detail and documentation, but it is limited to England and Wales in the first half of the twentieth century and thus has relevance to our topic only as a comparative study of similar cultures. Wilson, *Murderess,* has similar limitations.

Chapter 1

1. This background section on sex bias in the death penalty system is based in large part upon my earlier work addressing this issue more directly. See Victor L. Streib, "Gendering the Death Penalty: Countering Sex Bias in a Masculine Sanctuary," *Ohio State Law Journal* 63, no. 1 (2002): 433–74; and Streib, "Death Penalty for Female Offenders," *University of Cincinnati Law Review* 58, no. 3 (1990): 845–80.

2. The leading scholar on gender bias in the death penalty system is Professor Elizabeth Rapaport at the University of New Mexico. See, e.g., "Capital Murder and the Domestic Discount: A Study of Capital Domestic Murder in the Post-Furman Era," *Southern Methodist University Law Review* 49 (July–August 1996): 1507–48; "The Death Penalty and Gender Discrimination," *Law and Society Review* 25, no. 2 (1991): 367–83; "Equality of the Damned: The Execution of Women on the Cusp of the 21st Century," *Ohio Northern Law Review* 26, no. 3 (2000): 581–600; "Some Questions about Gender and the Death Penalty," *Golden Gate University Law Review* 20 (Fall 1990): 501–65; and "Staying Alive: Executive Clemency, Equal Protection, and the Politics of Gender in Women's Capital Cases," *Buffalo Criminal Law Review* 4, no. 2 (2001): 967–1007.

Another top scholar on this and related issues is Joan W. Howarth at the University of Nevada at Las Vegas. See, e.g., "Deciding to Kill: Revealing the Gender in the Task Handed to Capital Jurors," *Wisconsin Law Review* 1994, no. 6:1345–1424; "Executing White Masculinities: Learning from Karla Faye Tucker," *Oregon Law Review* 81 (Spring 2002): 183–229; and "Feminism, Lawyering, and Death Row," *Southern California Review of Law and Women's Studies* 2 (Fall 1992): 401–25.

Others have also made significant contributions on this issue, broadly defined. See particularly Anette Ballinger, *Dead Woman Walking: Executed Women in England and Wales 1900–1955* (Aldershot, England: Ashgate, 2000); Phyllis L. Crocker, "Is the Death Penalty Good for Women?" *Buffalo Criminal Law Review* 4, no. 2 (2001): 917–65; L. Kay Gillespie, *Dancehall Ladies: Executed Women of the 20th Century* (Lanham, Md.: University Press of America, 2000); Bernard O'Donnell, *Should Women Hang?* (London: W. H. Allen, 1956); Kathleen A. O'Shea, *Women and the Death Penalty in the United States, 1900–1998* (Westport, Conn.: Praeger, 1999); Lorraine Schmall, "Forgiving Guin Garcia: Women, the Death Penalty and Commutation," *Wisconsin Women's Law Journal* 11, no. 2 (1996): 283–326; and Patrick Wilson, *Murderess: A Study of Women Executed in Britain since 1843* (London: Michael Joseph, 1971). Excellent student work has included Jenny E. Carroll, "Images of Women and Capital Sentencing among Female Offenders: Exploring the Outer Limits of the Eighth Amendment and Articulated Theories of Justice," *Texas Law Review* 75 (May 1997): 1413–53; Janice L. Kopec, "Avoiding a Death Sentence in the American Legal System: Get a Woman to Do It," *Capital Defense Journal* 15 (Spring 2003): 353–82; Melinda E. O'Neil, "The Gender Gap Arguments: Exploring the Disparity of Sentencing Women to Death," *New England Journal of Criminal and Civil Confinement* 25 (Winter 1999): 213–44; and Andrea Shapiro, "Unequal before the Law: Men, Women and the Death Penalty," *American University Journal of Gender, Social Policy and Law* 8, no. 2 (2000): 427–70.

The author helped to begin this discussion fifteen years ago and to spread it to a broader audience. See, e.g., Victor L. Streib, "Death Penalty for Battered Women," *Florida State Law Review* 20 (Summer 1992): 163–94; "Death Penalty for Female Offenders," *University of Cincinnati Law Review* 58, no. 3 (1990): 845–80; "Death Penalty for Lesbians," *National Journal of Sexual Orientation Law* 1, no. 1 (1995): 104–26, http://www.ibiblio.org/gaylaw/issue1/streib.html; "Executing Women, Children, and the Retarded: Second Class Citizenship in Capital Punishment," in *America's Experiment with Capital Punishment: Reflections on the Past, Present and Future of the Ultimate Penal Sanction,* ed. James R. Acker, Robert M. Bohm, and Charles S. Lanier, 2d ed. (Durham, N.C.: Carolina Academic, 1998; 2d ed. 2003), 301–23; "Death Penalty for Female Offenders" (quarterly Web report), http://www.law.onu.edu/faculty/streib/streib.htm; "Gendering the Death Penalty"; and Victor L. Streib and Lynn Sametz, "Executing Juvenile Females," *Connecticut Law Review* 22 (Fall 1989): 3–59.

3. See, e.g., Rapaport, "Equality of the Damned" and "Death Penalty," as compared to Streib, "Gendering the Death Penalty" and "Death Penalty for Female Offenders" (*U. Cin. L. Rev.*).

4. Justice Thurgood Marshall observed that "[t]here is also overwhelming evidence that the death penalty is employed against men and not women. Only 32 women have been executed since 1930, while 3,827 men have met a similar fate. It is difficult to understand why women have received such favored treatment since

the purposes allegedly served by capital punishment seemingly are applicable to both sexes." Furman v. Georgia, 408 U.S. 238, 365 (1972) (Marshall, J., concurring) (footnotes omitted).

5. Howarth, "Deciding to Kill," 1347.

6. Ibid., 1350.

7. Streib, "Gendering the Death Penalty," 437.

8. See, e.g., Tison v. Arizona, 481 U.S. 137 (1987); and Coker v. Georgia, 433 U.S. 584 (1977).

9. For a particularly persuasive piece on this issue, see Rapaport, "Capital Murder."

10. See Richard A. Rosen, "Felony Murder and the Eighth Amendment Jurisprudence of Death," *Boston College Law Review* 31 (September 1990): 1103–70.

11. See Rapaport, "Capital Murder."

12. See Streib, "Gendering the Death Penalty," 458–59.

13. For the author's general discussion of these factors, see Victor L. Streib, *Death Penalty in a Nutshell,* 2d ed. (St. Paul, Minn.: Thomson West, 2005), 69–92.

14. Roger Hood, *The Death Penalty: A World-Wide Perspective,* rev. ed. (Oxford: Clarendon, 1996), 22, 91–92.

15. See, e.g., 18 U.S.C. § 3592(c)(9) (2000); Ariz. Rev. Stat. § 13-703(F)(4) (2001 & Supp. 2005); Ga. Code Ann. § 17-10-30(b)(6) (2004); Ohio Rev. Code Ann. § 2929.04(A)(2) (West 2005).

16. Ohio Rev. Code Ann. § 2929.04(A)(2) (West 2005).

17. See, e.g., Ohio Rev. Code Ann. §§ 2929.04(A)(5) and (B)(5) (West 2005).

18. See Streib, "Gendering the Death Penalty," 461.

19. See, e.g., 18 U.S.C. § 3592(c)(1) (2000); Ariz. Rev. Stat. §§ 13-1105(A)(2) and (B) (2001 & Supp. 2005); Ga. Code Ann. § 17-10-30(b)(2) (2004); Ohio Rev. Code Ann. § 2929.04(A)(7) (West 2005).

20. See Rosen, "Felony Murder."

21. See, e.g., 18 U.S.C. § 3592(c)(9) (2000); Cal. Penal Code § 190.2(a)(15) (West 1999); Ohio Rev. Code Ann. § 2929.04(A)(7) (West 2005).

22. 18 U.S.C. § (3592)(c)(9) (2000).

23. See Streib, "Gendering the Death Penalty" and "Death Penalty for Female Offenders" (*U. Cin. L. Rev.*).

24. See, e.g., 18 U.S.C. §§ 3592(a)(2) and (6) (2000); Ariz. Rev. Stat. § 13-703(G)(2) (2001 & Supp. 2005); Cal. Penal Code § 190.3(d) (West 1999); Ohio Rev. Code Ann. §§ 2929.04(B)(2) and (3) (West 2005).

25. Cal. Penal Code § 190.3(d) (West 1999).

26. Ohio Rev. Code Ann. § 2929.04(B)(2) (West 2005).

27. See Streib, "Gendering the Death Penalty" and "Death Penalty for Female Offenders" (*U. Cin. L. Rev.*).

28. See, e.g., 18 U.S.C. §§ 3592(A)(2) and (3) (2000); Cal. Penal Code § 190.3(g) (West 1999); Ohio Rev. Code Ann. § 2929.04(B)(6) (West 2005).

29. Cal. Penal Code § 190.3(g) (West 1999).

30. See, e.g., 18 U.S.C. § 3592(a)(8) (2000); Ariz. Rev. Stat. § 13–703(G) (2001 & Supp. 2005); Cal. Penal Code § 190.3(k) (West 1999); Ohio Rev. Code Ann. § 2929.04(B)(7) (West 2005).

31. Ohio Rev. Code Ann. § 2929.04(B)(7) (West 2005).

32. Eddings v. Oklahoma, 455 U.S. 104 (1982); and Lockett v. Ohio, 438 U.S. 586 (1978).

Chapter 2

1. This chapter is based largely on Victor L. Streib, "Death Penalty for Female Offenders" (quarterly Web report), http://www.law.onu.edu/faculty/streib/streib .htm.

2. Almost all nonmurder crimes (e.g., rape, robbery) that historically were eligible for the death penalty have been rejected in the current era. Coker v. Georgia, 433 U.S. 584 (1977). Essentially, the only remaining nonmurder death penalty crimes are treason and espionage. Victor L. Streib, *Death Penalty in a Nutshell,* 2d ed. (St. Paul, Minn.: Thomson West, 2005), 64–68.

3. See chapter 5.

4. See chapter 1 and Streib, *Death Penalty in a Nutshell,* 108–12.

5. Streib, *Death Penalty in a Nutshell,* 108–12.

6. Streib, "Death Penalty for Female Offenders" (*U. Cin. L. Rev.*).

7. Victor L. Streib, "American Executions of Female Offenders: An Inventory of Names, Dates, and Other Information," 7th ed. (unpublished research report on file with author, July 1, 2005).

8. See table 5.1, chapter 5.

9. Streib, *Death Penalty in a Nutshell,* 6–8.

10. Furman v. Georgia, 408 U.S. 238 (1972).

11. Gregg v. Georgia, 428 U.S. 153 (1976).

12. Victor L. Streib, *Death Penalty for Juveniles* (Bloomington: Indiana University Press, 1987), 89–90; and Victor L. Streib and Lynn Sametz, "Executing Juvenile Females," *Connecticut Law Review* 22 (Fall 1989): 3–59.

13. Jeff Eckhoff, "Jury Calls for Johnson's Death," *Des Moines (Iowa) Register,* June 22, 2005.

14. See appendix, "Case Summaries for Female Offenders under Death Sentences as of December 31, 2005."

Chapter 3

1. For an entertaining sketch of this issue, see Eugene G. Wanger, "Capital Punishment in Ohio: A Brief History," *Ohio Lawyer,* November–December 2002, 8, 11, 30. For a more factually detailed brief history, see Ohio Department of Re-

habilitation and Correction, "Capital Punishment in Ohio," http://www.drc.state
.oh.us/public/capital.htm. See also Office of the Attorney General of Ohio, "Capital Crimes Annual Report; 2003 Update—State and Federal Cases" (April 1, 2004), 1, http://www.ag.state.oh.us/online_publications/capital_crimes/annual_report _capital _crimes_2004.pdf.

2. Furman v. Georgia, 408 U.S. 238, 305 (1972) (Brennan, J., concurring). See also Raul Berger, *Death Penalties: The Supreme Court's Obstacle Course* (Cambridge: Harvard University Press, 1982), 43–47. See Stuart Banner, *The Death Penalty: An American History* (Cambridge: Harvard University Press, 2002); and John Laurence, *The History of Capital Punishment* (Secaucus, N.J.: Citadel, 1960).

3. Gregg v. Georgia, 428 U.S. 153, 177 (1976) (Stewart, J., plurality).

4. *Laws Passed in the Territory of the United States North-West of the River Ohio* (Philadelphia: Printed by F. Childs and J. Swaine, 1788; microfiche, Buffalo, N.Y.: Hein, 1986), chap. 6, 17–19.

5. The treason statute refers to potential defendants as "any person" and "the person or persons so offending." Ibid., 17–18. The murder statute refers to offenders as "any person or persons." Ibid., 18. The arson statute uses similar language: "And in case death should ensue from such burning, the offender or offenders upon conviction thereof, shall suffer the pains of death." Ibid., 19.

6. The punishment for treason, in addition to death, included the forfeiture of "his, her or their estate, real or personal, to this territory." Ibid., 18. Both the murder statute and the arson statute used the language "he, she or they so offending." Ibid., 18 and 19.

7. Ibid., 18 (emphasis added).

8. U.S. Const. amend. VI (emphasis added).

9. U.S. Const. art. IV, § 2, cl. 2 (emphasis added).

10. U.S. Const. amend. V (emphasis added).

11. 3 Laws of Ohio 1–2 (1805).

12. Ibid., 2 (emphasis added).

13. Ibid., 3.

14. Ibid., 2 (emphasis added).

15. 13 Laws of Ohio 87 (1814).

16. Ibid., 90–91.

17. Ibid., 85–86.

18. Ibid., 86 (emphasis added).

19. Ibid., 102 (emphasis added).

20. Ibid., 104 (emphasis added).

21. 13 Laws of Ohio 2 (1805).

22. See, e.g., "The History of the Death Penalty in Ohio," http://www .ohiodeathrow.com.

23. Hester Foster was hanged in Columbus, Ohio, on February 9, 1844. See Alfred Emery Lee, *History of the City of Columbus, Capital of Ohio* (New York: Munsell, 1892), 2:581; and chapter 6.

Chapter 4

1. 82 Laws of Ohio 169 (1885). See also Eugene G. Wanger, "Capital Punishment in Ohio: A Brief History," *Ohio Lawyer,* November–December 2002, 8, 11, 30.

2. 93 Laws of Ohio 223 (1898).

3. See chapters 8, 9, and 10.

4. All death penalty jurisdictions were forced to completely rewrite their death penalty statutes as a result of the holdings in Lockett v. Ohio, 438 U.S. 586 (1978); Gregg v. Georgia, 428 U.S. 153 (1976); and Furman v. Georgia, 408 U.S. 238 (1972). See Jack A. Guttenberg, "Recent Changes in Ohio Sentencing Law: The Questions Left Unanswered," *University of Toledo Law Review* 15 (Fall 1983): 35–69; David J. Benson, "Constitutionality of Ohio's New Death Penalty Statute," *University of Toledo Law Review* 14 (Fall 1982): 77–97; Elaine C. Hilliard, "Capital Punishment in Ohio: Aggravating Circumstances," *Cleveland State Law Review* 31, no. 3 (1982): 495–528; Anthony L. Geiger and Scott Selbach, "S.B. 1: Ohio Enacts Death Penalty Statute," *University of Dayton Law Review* 7 (Spring 1982): 531–66; William H. Hart, "Capital Punishment in Ohio: The Constitutionality of the Death Penalty Statute," *University of Dayton Law Review* 3 (Winter 1978): 169–96; Susan M. Kuzma, "The Constitutionality of Ohio's Death Penalty," *Ohio State Law Journal* 38, no. 3 (1977): 617–75; Jeffrey T. Heintz, "Legislative Response to Furman v. Georgia—Ohio Restores the Death Penalty," *Akron Law Review* 8 (Fall 1974): 149–61; and Kathryn Haller, "Capital Punishment Statutes after Furman," *Ohio State Law Journal* 35, no. 3 (1974): 651–85.

5. See part IV.

6. Furman v. Georgia, 408 U.S. 238 (1972).

7. State v. Leigh, Ohio St. 2d 97, 285 N.E.2d 333 (1972).

8. Ohio Rev. Code Ann. §§ 2929.01 et. seq. (Page 1975). See Heintz, "Legislative Response"; and Haller, "Capital Punishment Statutes."

9. See chapters 10, 11, 12, and 13.

10. Lockett v. Ohio, 438 U.S. 586 (1978).

11. Ohio Rev. Code § 2929.02 (Page 1982). See Benson, "Constitutionality of Ohio's New Death Penalty Statute."

12. Ohio Rev. Code § 2929.02(A).

13. Ohio Rev. Code § 2929.022(A) (emphasis added).

14. Ohio Rev. Code § 2929.023 (emphasis added).

15. See ibid., in combination with Ohio Rev. Code § 2929.03(D)(1).

16. See Victor L. Streib, "Capital Punishment of Children in Ohio: 'They'd Never Send a Boy of Seventeen to the Chair in Ohio, Would They?'" *Akron Law Review* 18 (Summer 1984): 51–102.

17. Ohio Rev. Code § 2929.11(C) (emphasis added).

18. Ohio Rev. Code § 2929.04(A)(2). See Streib, "Gendering the Death Penalty" and "Death Penalty for Female Offenders" (*U. Cin. L. Rev.*).

19. Ohio Rev. Code § 2929.04(A)(9).

20. Ohio Rev. Code § 2929.04(A)(7).

21. Ohio Rev. Code §§ 2929.04(B)(2) and 2929.04(B)(5).

22. Ohio Rev. Code § 2929.04(B)(6).

23. See chapters 14–20.

Chapter 5

1. See, e.g., Watt Espy, "List of Confirmations, State-by-State, of Legal Executions as of August 10, 1998" (unpublished report, Capital Punishment Research Project, August 1998). The research of Mr. Espy, director of the Capital Punishment Research Project, on American executions is highly respected. See also William J. Bowers, *Legal Homicide: Death as Punishment in America, 1864–1982* (Boston: Northeastern University Press, 1984), xxvi, xxviii, 395–97; and Victor L. Streib, *Death Penalty for Juveniles* (Bloomington: Indiana University Press, 1987), x.

2. Eugene G. Wanger, "Capital Punishment in Ohio: A Brief History," *Ohio Lawyer,* November–December 2002, 8, 11, 30.

3. Ibid.; Ohio Department of Rehabilitation and Correction, "Capital Punishment in Ohio," http://www.drc.state.oh.us/public/capital.htm.

4. H. M. Fogle, *The Palace of Death; or, The Ohio Penitentiary Annex* (Columbus, Ohio: privately printed, 1908), 1. The last person hanged there or anywhere in Ohio was William Paul on April 29, 1896. Ibid., 130–33.

5. Ibid., 136–42. The first Ohio prisoner to die in the electric chair was William Haas on April 21, 1897. See ibid., 136, and Victor L. Streib, "Capital Punishment of Children in Ohio: 'They'd Never Send a Boy of Seventeen to the Chair in Ohio, Would They?'" *Akron Law Review* 18 (Summer 1984), 71–72.

6. This information, in wonderful detail, can be found in Bowers, *Legal Homicide,* 479–86.

Chapter 6

1. Alfred Emory Lee, *History of the City of Columbus, Capital of Ohio* (New York: Munsell, 1892), 2:581; "A Woman Condemned to Be Hung in Ohio," *Raleigh Register and North Carolina Gazette,* January 12, 1844.

2. Esther, according to Lee, *History of the City,* 2:581; and "Women Should Take Medicine Like Men, Penologist Declares," *Cincinnati Enquirer,* November 9, 1937. Helen, according to "Woman Condemned to Be Hung in Ohio." Hester, according to "The Execution," *Cleveland Plain Dealer,* February 14, 1844.

3. Lee, *History of the City,* 2:581.

4. "Woman Condemned to Be Hung in Ohio."

5. Ibid.

6. David Lore, "The Pen," *Columbus Dispatch Magazine,* October 28, 1984, 10.

7. "Execution."

8. Lore, "Pen."

9. "Execution."

10. Lee, *History of the City,* 2:581.

11. "Execution."

12. Lee, *History of the City,* 2:581.

13. Ibid.; Lore, "Pen."

14. Lee, *History of the City,* 2:581.

15. Lore, "Pen."

Chapter 7

1. "Hahn Death Set for December 7," *Cincinnati Enquirer,* November 17, 1938.

2. "Interview Is Off, Then Mrs. Hahn Relents," *Cincinnati Enquirer,* August 18, 1937; "Death Chair Seals Lips of Blond Slayer; Events of Early Life to Remain a Mystery," *Cincinnati Enquirer,* December 8, 1938.

3. "Anna Hahn's Death Cell Confession! Four Cincinnati Murders Are Laid Bare," *Cincinnati Enquirer,* December 19, 1938.

4. Ibid.

5. "Death Chair."

6. "Anna Hahn's Death Cell."

7. "Interview Is Off."

8. "Anna Hahn Arrived in City on Uncle's $236, Not $16,000," *Cincinnati Enquirer,* August 17, 1937.

9. "Anna Hahn's Death Cell"; "Death Chair"; "Interview Is Off"; "Philip Hahn Submits to Interview on Courtship, Marriage Details," *Cincinnati Enquirer,* August 14, 1937.

10. "Anna Hahn's Death Cell."

11. "Philip Hahn."

12. "Interview Is Off."

13. "Anna Hahn's Death Cell."

14. Ibid.

15. "Death Chair."

16. Jay Robert Nash, *Look for the Woman: A Narrative Encyclopedia of Female Poisoners, Kidnappers, Thieves, Terrorists, Swindlers and Spies from Elizabethan Times to the Present* (London: Harrap Publishers, 1984), 178–79.

17. Kerry Segrave, *Women Serial and Mass Murderers: A Worldwide Reference, 1580 through 1990* (Jefferson, N.C.: McFarland, 1993), 164.

18. Nash, *Look for the Woman,* 178–79.

19. Segrave, *Women Serial and Mass Murderers,* 164, 162.

20. State v. Hahn, 10 Ohio Op. 29 (1937).

21. Segrave, *Women Serial and Mass Murderers,* 162.

22. "Police Grill 'Nurse Friend' of Mystery Death Victims," *Cincinnati Enquirer,* August 12, 1937.

23. "Death Chair."

24. Ibid.

25. Ibid.

26. Charles Walker, "Angel of Mercy—or Angel of Death," *True Detective,* July 1973, 47.

27. "Death Chair."

28. Ibid.

29. Walker, "Angel of Mercy."

30. "Death Chair."

31. State v. Hahn, 10 Ohio Op. 29 (1937).

32. "Death Chair."

33. Walker, "Angel of Mercy."

34. "Death Chair."

35. Ibid.

36. Walker, "Angel of Mercy."

37. "Death Chair."

38. "Hahn Trial Is to Open Today," *Cincinnati Enquirer,* October 11, 1937.

39. "Seven Jurors Chosen in Hahn Murder Trial; Death Penalty Hinted," *Cincinnati Enquirer,* October 12, 1937.

40. "Murder Jury Is Still Incomplete; Ten Women in Tentative Panel after Night Session of Hahn Trial," *Cincinnati Enquirer,* October 14, 1937.

41. "Hahn Jury Completed; Eleven Women Chosen; Hearing Begins Today," *Cincinnati Enquirer,* October 15, 1937.

42. "Seven Jurors."

43. "Wagner's Physician Testifies in Hahn Case," *Cincinnati Enquirer,* October 16, 1937.

44. "Wagner's Death Is Described by Physicians and Nurses," *Cincinnati Enquirer,* October 17, 1937.

45. "Wagner and Palmer Poisoned, Report Defense Expert; Gsellman's Death Story Begun," *Cincinnati Enquirer,* October 26, 1937.

46. "Wagner's 'Will' Forged by Anna Hahn," *Cincinnati Enquirer,* October 28, 1937.

47. "Woman Found Poisons in Wagner's Dwelling, Hahn Trial Testimony," *Cincinnati Enquirer,* October 19, 1937.

48. Ibid.; "To Kill Four, Jury Is Told; Defense Is to Call Expert," *Cincinnati Enquirer,* October 20, 1937.

49. "To Kill Four."

50. "Anna Hahn's Trial Halted Temporarily over Question of Embalming Powder," *Cincinnati Enquirer,* October 21, 1937.

51. "Dispute Delays Hahn Trial, Scope of Evidence Argued," *Cincinnati Enquirer,* October 22, 1937.

52. "Trial Marks Anna Hahn," *Cincinnati Enquirer,* October 23, 1937.

53. "Anna Hahn on Stand in Own Defense; Son Is also to Testify," *Cincinnati Enquirer,* November 1, 1937.

54. "Closing Arguments Today," *Cincinnati Enquirer,* November 4, 1937.

55. "Lies, All Lies Anna Hahn Exclaims under State Grilling in Murder Case," *Cincinnati Enquirer,* November 2, 1937.

56. "Anna Hahn on Stand."

57. "Lies, All Lies."

58. "Closing Arguments."

59. "Anna Hahn's Fate in Jury's Hands," *Cincinnati Enquirer,* November 6, 1937.

60. "Closing Arguments."

61. "To Die for Murder," *Cincinnati Enquirer,* November 7, 1937.

62. "Attorney Asks for New Trial," *Cincinnati Enquirer,* November 9, 1937.

63. "March 10 Set as Death Date for Blond German Slayer; Anna Hahn Faints in Cell," *Cincinnati Enquirer,* November 28, 1937.

64. Ibid.

65. State v. Hahn, 59 Ohio App. 178, 17 N.E.2d 392 (1938).

66. "Hahn Death Set."

67. "Hahn Plea Put before Davey," *Cincinnati Enquirer,* November 18, 1938.

68. Ibid.

69. "Anna Hahn Either Innocent or Insane, Attorney Avers in Final Appeal for Mercy," *Cincinnati Enquirer,* December 2, 1938.

70. "Son Visits Mrs. Anna Hahn as Davey's Aide Prepares Report on Mercy Plea," *Cincinnati Enquirer,* December 6, 1938.

71. "Anna Hahn to Die Tonight," *Cincinnati Enquirer,* December 7, 1938.

72. "Anna Hahn Falls and Is Carried to Chair; Dies after She Cries Appeal to Spectators," *Cincinnati Enquirer,* December 8, 1938.

73. Ibid.

74. "Read Anna Marie Hahn's Sensational Confession in Monday, Tuesday Enquirer," *Cincinnati Enquirer,* December 18, 1938.

75. "Hahn Letters in Safe at Home for Several Days, Hoodin Says; Boy's Care in Attorneys' Hands," *Cincinnati Enquirer,* December 9, 1938.

76. "Hahn Letters," *Cincinnati Enquirer,* December 14, 1938.

77. "All Doubt of Blonde's Guilt Dissipated by Confession Penned in Prison Cell," *Cincinnati Enquirer,* December 19, 1938.

78. "Poison Death Details Bared," *Cincinnati Enquirer,* December 20, 1938.

79. "All Doubt."

80. "Lies, All Lies."

81. Nash, *Look for the Woman,* 178.

82. "Death Chair."

83. "Anna Hahn Falls."

84. "Death Chair."

85. "Trial Marks."

86. "Anna Hahn's Death Cell."

87. "Death Chair."

88. See, e.g., "March 10 Set."

89. See "Anna Hahn's Death Cell."

90. "Death Chair."

Chapter 8

1. "Mrs. Dean's Murder Trial to Begin October 20; Will Cost County $4,000," *Batavia (Ohio) Clermont Sun,* September 25, 1952; "Stepson Released as Officials Probe Death of Farmer," *Batavia (Ohio) Clermont Courier,* September 11, 1952.

2. "Mrs. Dean Faces Murder Charge," *Batavia (Ohio) Clermont Sun,* September 18, 1952; "Three Poisonings Cases; Investigator Is Named," *Batavia (Ohio) Clermont Sun,* September 4, 1952.

3. "Prosecution Files Brief in Dean Case," *Batavia (Ohio) Clermont Courier,* April 9, 1953.

4. "Defense Fights Murder Confession," *Batavia (Ohio) Clermont Sun,* December 11, 1952.

5. Ibid.

6. "Arsenic Poisoning Reported," *Batavia (Ohio) Clermont Courier,* August 28, 1952.

7. "Defense Fights"; "Given Reprieve by Governor Lausche," *Batavia (Ohio) Clermont Courier,* November 5, 1953; "Mrs. Dean Unemotional as Murder Trial Opens," *Batavia (Ohio) Clermont Courier,* December 11, 1952; "Widow Confesses Poisoning Elderly Mate after Trying to Fasten Crime upon Her Son," *Cincinnati Enquirer,* September 13, 1952.

8. "Mrs. Dean Faces."

9. "Arsenic Poisoning Reported"; "Defense Fights."

10. "Mrs. Dean Not Now Sane, Defense Attorneys Claim; Trial Is Delayed," *Batavia (Ohio) Clermont Sun,* October 9, 1952; "Stepson Released."

11. "Arsenic Poisoning Reported."

12. "Mrs. Dean Unemotional"; "Widow Confesses."

13. "Arsenic Poisoning Reported."

14. Ibid.; "Mrs. Dean Unemotional"; "Three Poisonings."

15. "Authorities Pursue Poison Probe," *Batavia (Ohio) Clermont Sun,* September 11, 1952.

16. Ibid.

17. "Officials Probe Death of Farmer," *Batavia (Ohio) Clermont Courier,* September 4, 1952.

18. "Three Poisonings"; "Widow Confesses."

19. "Widow Confesses."

20. "Judge's Ruling Awaited on Dean New Trial Motion," *Batavia (Ohio) Clermont Courier,* January 11, 1953.

21. "Defense Fights"; "Mrs. Dean Faces"; "Mrs. Dean Unemotional."

22. "Widow Confesses."

23. "Mrs. Dean Unemotional."

24. "Defense Fights"; "Widow Confesses."

25. "Defense Fights."

26. "Widow Confesses."

27. Ibid.; "Poison Murder Trial to Begin Dec. 8," *Batavia (Ohio) Clermont Sun,* November 20, 1952.

28. "Mrs. Dean Unemotional."

29. "Widow Confesses."

30. "Mrs. Dean Faces"; "Woman Indicted on First Degree Murder Charge," *Batavia (Ohio) Clermont Courier,* September 18, 1952.

31. "Mrs. Dean Faces"; "Mrs. Dean's Murder Trial"; "Murder Trial Date Set for Mrs. Dovie Dean Is Oct. 20," *Batavia (Ohio) Clermont Courier,* September 25, 1952.

32. "Mrs. Dean's Murder Trial."

33. Ibid.; "Murder Trial Date."

34. "Mrs. Dean Not Now Sane"; "Sanity Test Ordered for Mrs. Dovie Dean in Poison Case," *Batavia (Ohio) Clermont Courier,* October 9, 1952.

35. "Mrs. Dean Not Now Sane."

36. "Mrs. Dean Ruled Sane by Common Pleas Court," *Batavia (Ohio) Clermont Courier,* November 20, 1952; "Mrs. Dean's Murder Trial Rescheduled," *Batavia (Ohio) Clermont Courier,* November 13, 1952; "Poison Murder Trial"; "Will Conduct Hearing on Mrs. Dean's Sanity Monday," *Batavia (Ohio) Clermont Sun,* November 13, 1952.

37. "Poison Murder Trial."

38. "Mrs. Dean's Murder Trial"; "Will Conduct Hearing."

39. "Murder Trial Begins Monday," *Batavia (Ohio) Clermont Sun,* December 4, 1952.

40. "Poison Murder Trial."

41. "Defense Fights."

42. "Mrs. Dean Unemotional."

43. "Defense Fights."

44. Ibid.; "Mrs. Dean Unemotional."

45. "Fight to Save Mrs. Dean from Chair," *Batavia (Ohio) Clermont Sun,* December 18, 1952.

46. "Mrs. Dean Unemotional."

47. "Fight to Save."

48. Ibid.

49. Ibid.

50. Ibid.; "Dean Verdict Appealed," *Batavia (Ohio) Clermont Courier,* December 18, 1952.

51. "Dean Verdict."

52. "Dovie Dean to Die June 5 in Electric Chair," *Batavia (Ohio) Clermont Courier,* February 26, 1953.

53. State v. Dean, 94 Ohio App. 540, 116 N.E.2d 767 (1953).

54. "Dovie Dean to Die."

55. "Appeals Court Reviewing Details of Dean Case," *Batavia (Ohio) Clermont Courier,* April 13, 1953.

56. "Dean Case Taken to First District Court of Appeals," *Batavia (Ohio) Clermont Courier,* March 26, 1953.

57. "Prosecution Files."

58. "Court Affirms Murder Verdict," *Batavia (Ohio) Clermont Courier,* May 21, 1953.

59. State v. Dean, 94 Ohio App. 540, 116 N.E.2d 767 (1953).

60. "Execution Date Set," *Batavia (Ohio) Clermont Courier,* October 8, 1953.

61. "Clemency Hearing for Mrs. Dean Set," *Batavia (Ohio) Clermont Courier,* October 15, 1953; "Clemency Hearing to Decide Fate of Dovie Dean," *Batavia (Ohio) Clermont Courier,* October 29, 1953.

62. "Clemency Hearing for Mrs. Dean Set"; "Clemency Hearing to Decide."

63. "Given Reprieve."

64. "Eyewitness Account of Dean Execution," *Batavia (Ohio) Clermont Courier,* January 21, 1954.

65. "Electric Chair Fails to Disturb Dovie Dean's Perfect Emotional Control in Last Moments," *Batavia (Ohio) Clermont Courier,* January 21, 1954.

66. "Eyewitness."

67. "Electric Chair."

68. "Eyewitness."

69. "Electric Chair."

70. "Eyewitness."

71. "Electric Chair."

72. "Eyewitness."

73. Ibid.; "Electric Chair."

74. "Electric Chair."

75. "Authorities Pursue."

76. "Poison Murder Trial"; "Widow Confesses."

77. "Mrs. Dean Not Now Sane"; "Stepson Released."

78. "Authorities Pursue."

79. "Mrs. Dean Not Now Sane."

80. "Fight to Save"; "Mrs. Dean Unemotional."

81. "Defense Fights."

Chapter 9

1. "Betty Butler Dies," *Cincinnati Enquirer,* June 12, 1954.

2. "West End Woman Strangled, Drowned in Sharon Woods," *Cincinnati Enquirer,* September 7, 1952.

3. "Betty Butler Dies."

4. Elizabeth Rapaport, "Some Questions about Gender and the Death Penalty," *Golden Gate University Law Review* 20 (Fall 1990): 525.

5. "West End Woman."

6. Rapaport, "Some Questions," 525.

7. "West End Woman."

8. "Rival Choked and Drowned, Woman Held for Grand Jury," *Cincinnati Enquirer,* September 8, 1952.

9. "West End Woman."

10. "Rival Choked."

11. "West End Woman."

12. "Rival Choked."

13. "West End Woman."

14. "Rival Choked."

15. Ibid.

16. Ibid.

17. "3d Woman Pays with Life in Ohio's Electric Chair," *Cleveland Plain Dealer,* June 12, 1954.

18. "Betty Butler Dies."

19. Ibid.; "3d Woman."

20. "Betty Butler Dies."

21. Ibid.

22. Ibid.

23. "3d Woman."

24. Ibid.; "Betty Butler Dies."

25. "Betty Butler Dies."

26. "Rival Choked."

27. "West End Woman."

28. Rapaport, "Some Questions," 525.

29. See Victor L. Streib, "Death Penalty for Lesbians," *National Journal of Sexual Orientation Law* 1, no. 1 (1995): 104–26, http://www.ibiblio.org/gaylaw/issue1/streib.html.

Chapter 10

1. Lockett v. Ohio, 438 U.S. 586, 589 (1978).

2. State v. Lockett, 49 Ohio St. 2d 48, 52, 358 N.E.2d 1062, 1066 (1976).

3. Lockett v. Ohio, 438 U.S. at 590.

4. State v. Lockett, 49 Ohio St. 2d at 52, 358 N.E.2d at 1067.

5. Lockett v. Ohio, 438 U.S. at 590.

6. Ibid., 591.

7. Ibid.

8. Ibid.

9. Ibid., 592.

10. State v. Lockett, 49 Ohio St. 2d at 54, 358 N.E.2d at 1067–68.

11. Lockett v. Ohio, 438 U.S. at 592.

12. Ibid., 593.

13. Ibid., 594.

14. State v. Lockett, 49 Ohio St. 2d at 48, 358 N.E.2d at 1062.

15. Ibid., 49 Ohio St. 2d at 56–62, 358 N.E.2d at 1069–72.

16. Ibid., 49 Ohio St. 2d at 65, 358 N.E.2d at 1073–74.

17. Lockett v. Ohio, 438 U.S. at 586.

18. Ibid., 587.

19. Ibid., 604.

20. Morton Mintz, "Three Major Court Rulings; Imposing Death Penalty Made Harder," *Washington Post,* July 4, 1978.

21. Debra Dennis, "Woman Who Broke Ohio Death Penalty Faces Prison Again," *Cleveland Plain Dealer,* March 5, 1997.

22. Lockett v. Ohio, 438 U.S. at 590.

23. Ibid.

24. Ibid., 589.

25. Ibid., 590.

Chapter 11

1. State v. Osborne, 49 Ohio St. 2d 135, 138, 359 N.E.2d 78, 81 (Ohio 1976).

2. Ibid.

3. Ibid.

4. Ibid., 49 Ohio St. 2d at 139, 359 N.E.2d at 82.

5. Ibid.

6. Ibid.

7. Ibid.

8. Ibid. 49 Ohio St. 2d at 135, 359 N.E.2d at 78.

9. Ibid. 49 Ohio St. 2d at 139–143, 359 N.E.2d at 82–86.

10. Ibid. 49 Ohio St. 2d at 135, 359 N.E.2d at 78.

11. Ibid. 49 Ohio St. 2d at 143, 359 N.E.2d at 86.

12. Lockett v. Ohio, 438 U.S. 586, 604–9 (1978).

13. Ibid., 604.

14. Ibid., 608.

15. State v. Osborne, 49 Ohio St. 2d at 138, 359 N.E.2d at 81.

16. Ibid., 49 Ohio St. 2d at 139, 359 N.E.2d at 82.

Chapter 12

1. "Two Juries Hear Opening Positions in Ottawa Hills Double Murder," *Toledo Blade,* September 14, 1976.

2. State v. Wernert, C.A. No. L-76-327, 1979 Ohio App. LEXIS 9325, *10 (6th Dist. May 25, 1979).

3. "Two Juries."

4. "Three Sentenced to Die in Double Slaying in Ottawa Hills," *Toledo Blade,* November 22, 1976.

5. "Son, His Wife, Second Man Charged with Murdering 2 Women in Ottawa Hills," *Toledo Blade,* November 28, 1975.

6. Wernert v. Wernert, 61 Ohio Misc. 2d 436, 444 (Ohio Com. Pl. 1991).

7. Patricia Wernert to Victor L. Streib, October 11, 1990 (letter on file with author).

8. Wernert v. Wernert, 61 Ohio Misc. 2d at 444.

9. Ibid., 437.

10. "Ottawa Hills Slaying Suspects Arraigned on Murder Charges," *Toledo Blade,* November 29, 1975.

11. "Two Women Found Beaten to Death in Ottawa Hills Home," *Toledo Blade,* November 20, 1975.

12. "Slayings in Ottawa Hills Believed Committed by at Least 2 Persons," *Toledo Blade,* November 21, 1975.

13. "Two Women."

14. "Slept before Killing Two Women, Arterberry Says in Recording," *Toledo Blade,* September 16, 1976.

15. "Two Juries."

16. "Slayings."

17. "Two Juries."

18. "Murders of Ottawa Hills Women Intended as Mercy Killings, Tape Played at Trial Says," *Toledo Blade,* September 15, 1976.

19. "Two Juries."

20. "Murders."

21. "Two Women."

22. "Son, His Wife."

23. Wernert v. Arn, 819 F.2d 613, 614 (6th Cir. 1987).

24. "Son, His Wife."

25. Wernert v. Arn, 819 F.2d at 614.

26. Ibid.

27. "Son, His Wife."

28. Wernert v. Arn, 819 F.2d at 614.

29. "Son, His Wife."

30. Wernert v. Arn, 819 F.2d at 614.

31. Ibid., 614–15.

32. Ibid., 615.

33. "Son, His Wife."

34. "Three Are Indicted in Slaying of Two at Ottawa Hills; Specifications Included Which Could Mean Use of Death Penalty," *Toledo Blade,* December 4, 1975.

35. "Accused Kin Is Beneficiary under 2 Wills," *Toledo Blade,* December 1, 1975.

36. "Murders."

37. "Accused Kin."

38. "Couple Enter Innocent Pleas to Charges of Murdering Kin," *Toledo Blade,* December 31, 1975.

39. "Britain Retains Death Penalty Ban," *Toledo Blade,* December 12, 1975.

40. Wernert to Streib.

41. "Taped Arrest Statements Ruled Admissible in Murder Trials," *Toledo Blade,* September 13, 1976.

42. Ibid.

43. Wernert v. Arn, 819 F.2d at 616.

44. "Taped Arrest Statements."

45. Ibid.

46. "Three Sentenced."

47. "Taped Arrest Statements."

48. Ibid.

49. "Two Juries."

50. "Murders."

51. "Slept before Killing."

52. "Murders."

53. "Slept before Killing."

54. "Murders."

55. "Slept before Killing."

56. "Arterberry Denies Killing Pair, Calls Confession to Police a Lie," *Toledo Blade,* September 18, 1976.

57. "Wernerts Accuse Each Other of Conspiring with Arterberry," *Toledo Blade,* September 17, 1976.

58. "Arterberry Denies."

59. "Slept before Killing."

60. Ibid.

61. Ibid.

62. "Arterberry Denies."

63. "Murders."

64. "Jury Deliberations Begin in Trials of 3 in Wernerts Case," *Toledo Blade,* September 20, 1976.

65. "Murders."

66. "Jury Deliberations."

67. "Sealed Verdicts Returned in Two of Ottawa Hills Murder Trials," *Toledo Blade,* September 21, 1976.

68. "Jury Deliberations."

69. "Sealed Verdicts."

70. "Death Penalty Hearing Scheduled November 22 for Wernerts, Arterberry," *Toledo Blade,* September 22, 1976.

71. "Sealed Verdicts."

72. "Death Penalty Hearing."

73. Ibid.

74. Ibid.

75. "Sealed Verdicts."

76. "Death Penalty Hearing."

77. "Three Sentenced."

78. Wernert to Streib.

79. State v. Wernert, 1979 Ohio App. LEXIS 9325, *1.

80. Ibid., *9.

81. Ibid., *6.

82. Ibid., *8.

83. Ibid., *9.

84. Ibid.

85. Ibid., *10.

86. Lockett v. Ohio, 438 U.S. 586 (1978).

87. State v. Wernert, 1979 Ohio App. LEXIS 9325, *10.

88. Lockett v. Ohio, 438 U.S. at 606.

89. Wernert to Streib.

90. State v. Wernert, 1979 Ohio App. LEXIS 9325, *10.

91. Wernert v. Ohio, 446 U.S. 942 (1980).

92. State v. Wernert, No. CR 75-7249B, 1982 WL 6371, *1, *3 (Ohio Ct. App. 6th Dist. Apr. 23, 1982).

93. Ibid., *1.

94. Ibid.

95. Ibid., *2.

96. Ibid.

97. State v. Wernert, No. CR 75-7249, 1984 WL 14306, *1 (Ohio Ct. App. 6th Dist. Oct. 19, 1984).

98. Wernert v. Arn, 819 F.2d 613, 614 (6th Cir. 1987).

99. Ibid., 619 (Enslen, J., dissenting).

100. Ibid., 614.

101. Ibid., 616.

102. Ibid., 618.

103. Ibid., 616.

104. Ibid., 617.

105. Poole v. Perini, 659 F.2d 730, 733 (6th Cir. 1981), *cert. denied,* 455 U.S. 910 (1982).

106. Wernert v. Arn, 819 F.2d at 617.

107. Ibid.

108. Wernert v. Arn, 819 F.2d at 617–18.

109. Wernert v. Arn, 484 U.S. 1011 (1988).

110. Wernert to Streib.

111. "Slept before Killing."

112. "Two Women."

113. "Slept before Killing."

Chapter 13

1. "Smiths Are Guilty in Holdup, Killing of Jules Vinnedge," *Toledo Blade,* September 11, 1977.

2. "Appeals Could Delay Execution of Pair under Death Sentence," *Toledo Blade,* December 1, 1977.

3. "Smiths Are Guilty."

4. "Benita Smith Role in Vinnedge Case Called a Major One," *Toledo Blade,* September 1, 1977.

5. "Jury Selection Starts in Vinnedge Case," *Toledo Blade,* August 29, 1977.

6. Ibid.

7. "Prosecution to Begin Presenting Case in the Vinnedge Murder Trial," *Toledo Blade,* August 31, 1977.

8. "Jury Selection."

9. "Prosecution to Begin."

10. "Benita Smith Role."

11. Ibid.

12. "Three at Scene of Vinnedge Slaying Unable to Identify Smith, Court Told," *Toledo Blade,* September 7, 1977.

13. "Benita Smith Role."

14. "Jury Told Vinnedge Murder Suspect Burned Lamson's Bag," *Toledo Blade,* September 2, 1977.

15. "Three at Scene."

16. "Jury Told."

17. Ibid.

18. "Vinnedge Only One in Charge on Day He Died, Clerk Testifies," *Toledo Blade,* September 6, 1977.

19. "Three at Scene."

20. "'Overwhelming' Doubt that Smith Shot Vinnedge Alleged in Closing Defense Arguments," *Toledo Blade,* September 9, 1977.

21. "Defense Rests in Theodore Smith Murder Trial, Prosecution Continues Evidence against Sister," *Toledo Blade,* September 8, 1977.

22. "Jurors in Benita Smith's Trial Slated to Begin Deliberations," *Toledo Blade,* September 10, 1977.

23. "Smiths Are Guilty."

24. "Appeals Could Delay."

25. Lockett v. Ohio, 438 U.S. 586 (1978).

26. Patricia Wernert to Victor L. Streib, October 11, 1990 (letter on file with the author).

27. State v. Smith, No. L-77-277 (Ohio Ct. App. 6th Dist. Feb. 16, 1979).

28. Wernert to Streib.

29. "Benita Smith Role"; "Smiths Are Guilty."

30. "Jury Told."

Chapter 14

1. State v. Young, No. C-870394, 1988 WL 85903, *1 (Ohio Ct. App. 1st Dist. Aug. 17, 1988).

2. Elizabeth Rapaport, "Some Questions about Gender and the Death Penalty," *Golden Gate University Law Review* 20 (Fall 1990): 533.

3. State v. Young, 1988 WL 85903, *1.

4. State v. Young, No. C-830757, 1986 WL 5503, *3 (Ohio Ct. App. 1st Dist. May 14, 1986).

5. State v. Young, 1988 WL 85903, *1.

6. Ibid.

7. State v. Young, 1986 WL 5503, *1.

8. State v. Young, 1988 WL 85903, *1.

9. State v. Young, 1986 WL 5503, *1.

10. Ibid., *4–16.

11. Ibid., *4–7.

12. Ibid., *5.

13. Ibid., *6.

14. Ibid.

15. Ibid., *7.

16. Ibid., *8.

17. Ibid., *9.

18. Ibid., *10.

19. Ibid., *7–13.

20. State v. Young, 1988 WL 85903, *1.

21. Ibid.

22. Ibid., *1–3.

23. Ibid., *1.

24. Ibid., *3.

25. State v. Young, 1986 WL 5503, *3.

26. Ibid.

27. State v. Young, 1988 WL 85903, *1.

28. Ibid.

29. Rapaport, "Some Questions," 533. See Victor L. Streib, "Death Penalty for Lesbians," *National Journal of Sexual Orientation Law* 1, no. 1 (1995): 104–26, http://www.ibiblio.org/gaylaw/issue1/streib.html.

Chapter 15

1. Randall M. Dana, "Background Information Provided," January 10, 1991 (press release from Public Defender for the State of Ohio, copy on file with author).

2. "Child Slayer Sentenced to Die," *Youngstown Vindicator*, October 22, 1983.

3. Tom Kuncl and Paul Einstein, *Ladies Who Kill* (New York: Pinnacle Books, 1985), 28.

4. "Child Slayer."

5. Kuncl and Einstein, *Ladies Who Kill,* 32.

6. Dana, "Background Information."

7. Kuncl and Einstein, *Ladies Who Kill,* 28–29.

8. Ibid., 25.

9. Ibid., 33.

10. "Jury Deciding if Miss Grant Is Guilty in Deaths of Her Two Children," *Youngstown Vindicator,* October 13, 1983.

11. Ibid.

12. Ibid.

13. "Death Possible for Miss Grant," *Youngstown Vindicator,* October 14, 1983.

14. Kuncl and Einstein, *Ladies Who Kill,* 43.

15. "Child Slayer."

16. Kuncl and Einstein, *Ladies Who Kill,* 44.

17. "Child Slayer."

18. "Death Possible."

19. "Child Slayer."

20. Dana, "Background Information."

21. State v. Grant, No. 83 C.A. 144, 1990 Ohio App. LEXIS 4949, *3 (7th Dist. Nov. 9, 1990).

22. Ibid., *3–108.

23. Ibid., *114–15.

24. Ibid., *115.

25. Ibid., *115–16.

26. State v. Grant, 67 Ohio St. 3d 465, 470, 620 N.E.2d 50, 59 (1993).

27. Ibid., 67 Ohio St. 3d at 484, 620 N.E.2d at 70.

28. Ibid., 67 Ohio St. 3d at 486, 620 N.E.2d at 71.

29. Ibid.

30. Ibid., 67 Ohio St. 3d at 486, 620 N.E.2d at 72.

31. Ibid., 67 Ohio St. 3d at 486, 620 N.E.2d at 71.

32. Ibid., 67 Ohio St. 3d at 486, 620 N.E.2d at 72.

33. State v. Grant, 68 Ohio St. 3d 1412, 623 N.E.2d 568 (1993).

34. Mary Beth Lane, "Celeste Commutes Eight Death Sentences," *Cleveland Plain Dealer,* January 11, 1991.

35. "Commuted Death Sentences Fought in Ohio," *New York Times,* January 30, 1991.

36. "State Questions Legal Issues in Pardons," *Cleveland Plain Dealer,* May 14, 1991.

37. Wilkinson v. Maurer, No. 91CVH-01-763, slip op., 12 (Franklin County Ct. Com. Pl. Feb. 13, 1992).

38. "Judge Voids Clemency for Eleven Prisoners," *Cleveland Plain Dealer,* February 14, 1992.

39. Wilkinson v. Maurer, No. 92AP-674, slip op., 30 (Ohio Ct. App. 10th Dist. April 8, 1993).

40. Kuncl and Einstein, *Ladies Who Kill,* 33; "Jury Deciding."

41. Kuncl and Einstein, *Ladies Who Kill,* 32; "Child Slayer."

42. Kuncl and Einstein, *Ladies Who Kill,* 44.

43. Ibid., 43.

Chapter 16

1. Randall M. Dana, "Background Information Provided," January 10, 1991 (press release from Public Defender for the State of Ohio, copy on file with author).

2. Janan Hanna, "Alton Coleman Ally Sought by Indiana," *Chicago Tribune,* January 12, 1991.

3. State v. Brown, No. C-850 434, 1987 WL 9743, *1 (Ohio Ct. App. 1st Dist. April 15, 1987).

4. State v. Brown, 38 Ohio St. 3d 305, 306, 528 N.E.2d 523, 528 (1988).

5. State v. Brown, 1987 WL 9743, *1.

6. State v. Brown, 38 Ohio St. 3d at 306, 528 N.E.2d at 529.

7. State v. Brown, 1987 WL 9743, *1.

8. Dana, "Background Information."

9. "Death Penalty Residents," Public Defender's Office, May–July 1991 (State Defender's Report).

10. Elizabeth Rapaport, "Some Questions about Gender and the Death Penalty," *Golden Gate University Law Review* 20 (Fall 1990): 554.

11. Dana, "Background Information."

12. Rapaport, "Some Questions," 554.

13. Dana, "Background Information."

14. Rapaport, "Some Questions," 554.

15. Dana, "Background Information."

16. State v. Brown, 38 Ohio St. 3d at 306, 528 N.E.2d at 529.

17. State v. Brown, 1987 WL 9743, *1.

18. Ibid., *2.

19. Ibid.

20. Ibid., *2–11.

21. Ibid., *2.

22. Ibid., *13.

23. State v. Brown, 38 Ohio St. 3d at 307, 528 N.E.2d at 529.

24. Ibid., 38 Ohio St. 3d at 307–21, 528 N.E.2d at 529–41.

25. Ibid., 38 Ohio St. 3d at 321, 528 N.E.2d at 542.

26. State v. Brown, 39 Ohio St. 3d 710, 534 N.E.2d 93 (Ohio 1988).

27. Ohio v. Brown, 489 U.S. 1040 (1989).

28. State ex rel. v. Brown v. Dana, 66 Ohio App. 3d 709, 586 N.E.2d 150 (1990).

29. Mary Beth Lane, "Celeste Commutes Eight Death Sentences," *Cleveland Plain Dealer,* January 11, 1991.

30. Hanna, "Alton Colman Ally."

31. Victor L. Streib, "Death Penalty for Female Offenders," October 3, 2005, 17 (quarterly Web report), http://www.law.onu.edu/faculty/streib/streib.htm.

32. Dana, "Background Information"; Rapaport, "Some Questions," 554.

33. Hanna, "Alton Coleman Ally."

34. Dana, "Background Information."

35. "Death Penalty Residents."

36. Rapaport, "Some Questions," 554.

37. Ibid.; Dana, "Background Information."

Chapter 17

1. Randall M. Dana, "Background Information Provided," January 10, 1991 (press release from Public Defender for the State of Ohio, on file with author).

2. Thrity Umrigar, "Living Life on Death Row; In Ohio, Two Women Try to Cope Each Day," *Akron Beacon Journal,* April 3, 1989.

3. Ibid.

4. Dana, "Background Information."

5. State v. Green, No. C-880 504, 1990 Ohio App. LEXIS 2798, *3 (July 11, 1990).

6. Ibid., *4.

7. Ibid., *5.

8. Ibid.

9. Ibid., *5–6.

10. Ibid., *5.

11. Ibid., *1–2.

12. Ibid., *2.

13. Ibid.

14. Ibid., *1.

15. Ibid., *6–10.

16. Ibid., *3.

17. Mary Beth Lane, "Celeste Commutes Eight Death Sentences," *Cleveland Plain Dealer,* January 11, 1991; "8 Death Sentences Commuted in Ohio," *New York Times,* January 12, 1991.

18. "Commuted Death Sentences Fought in Ohio," *New York Times,* January 30, 1991; Jim Underwood, "State Questions Legal Issues in Pardons," *Cleveland Plain Dealer,* May 14, 1991; "Ohio Judge Overturns Clemency Granted to Death-Row Prisoners," *New York Times,* February 16, 1991; Barry Kawa, "2 Sides to Argue 7 Killers' Fates," *Cleveland Plain Dealer,* September 19, 1994.

19. Lane, "Celeste Commutes."

20. State v. Green, 66 Ohio St. 3d 141, 154, 609 N.E.2d 1253, 1264 (1993).

21. Ibid., 1264 (Wright, J., concurring).

22. Ibid., 1264–65 (Pfeifer, J., dissenting).

23. Ohio v. Green, 510 U.S. 891 (1993).

24. Umrigar, "Living Life."

25. State v. Green, 1990 Ohio App. LEXIS 2798, *1–6.

26. State v. Green, 66 Ohio St. 3d at 154, 609 N.E.2d at 1264 (Pfeifer, J., dissenting).

27. Umrigar, "Living Life."

28. See Atkins v. Virginia, 536 U.S. 304 (2002) (holding death penalty unconstitutional for mentally retarded offenders).

Chapter 18

1. Randall M. Dana, "Background Information Provided," January 10, 1991 (press release from Public Defender for the State of Ohio, copy on file with author); Thrity Umrigar, "Living Life on Death Row: In Ohio, Two Women Try to Cope Each Day," *Akron Beacon Journal,* April 3, 1989.

2. Dana, "Background Information."

3. Ellen Sweets, "Women Facing Death Penalty in Increasing Numbers," *Dallas Morning News,* May 9, 1991.

4. State v. Lampkin, No. C-890273, 1990 Ohio App. LEXIS 4315, *3 (1st Dist. Oct. 3, 1990).

5. Ibid., *3–4.

6. Ibid., *4.

7. Ibid., *1–2.

8. Ibid., *2.

9. Dana, "Background Information."

10. State v. Lampkin, 1990 Ohio App. LEXIS 4315, *2.

11. Mary Beth Lane, "Celeste Commutes Eight Death Sentences," *Cleveland Plain Dealer,* January 11, 1991; Jim Underwood, "State Questions Legal Issues in Pardons," *Cleveland Plain Dealer,* May 14, 1991.

12. Sweets, "Women Facing Death Penalty."

13. "Ohio Woman Put to Death in '54," *Mansfield (Ohio) News Journal,* February 4, 1998.

14. Ohio Department of Rehabilitation and Correction, Offender Data, Beatrice Lampkin—W 025931 (Offender Information Database accessible at http://www.drc.state.oh.us).

15. State v. Lampkin, 1990 Ohio App. LEXIS 4315, *3.

16. Dana, "Background Information."

17. Ibid.; State v. Lampkin, 1990 Ohio App. LEXIS 4315, *3–4.

18. State v. Lampkin, 1990 Ohio App. LEXIS 4315, *3–4.

19. Wayne R. LaFave, *Principles of Criminal Law* (St. Paul, Minn.: Thomson West, 2003), 407–13.

Chapter 19

1. Peggy Sinkovich, "Roberts' Lawyers Consider Appeal; The Defendant Thanked the Judge after She Received the Death Penalty," *Youngstown (Ohio) Vindicator,* June 24, 2003; Sinkovich, "Lawyers Want Statement to Be Thrown Out," *Youngstown (Ohio) Vindicator,* April 18, 2002.

2. Peggy Sinkovich, "2 Jailed, Charged in Man's Slaying," *Youngstown (Ohio) Vindicator,* December 21, 2001.

3. Peggy Sinkovich, "Man Is Found Shot Dead in Home," *Youngstown (Ohio) Vindicator,* December 12, 2001.

4. Peggy Sinkovich, "Charge of Gun Theft Is Dismissed," *Youngstown (Ohio) Vindicator,* January 10, 2002.

5. Ibid.; Sinkovich, "Man Is Found."

6. Sinkovich, "Lawyers Want Statement"; Sinkovich, "Charge of Gun Theft."

7. Sinkovich, "Man is Found."

8. Peggy Sinkovich, "Police Search Car of Man Found Slain," *Youngstown (Ohio) Vindicator,* December 13, 2001.

9. Sinkovich, "Man Is Found."

10. Peggy Sinkovich, "Letters Reveal Scheme," *Youngstown (Ohio) Vindicator,* January 1, 2002.

11. Sinkovich, "Police Search Car."

12. Sinkovich, "Charge of Gun Theft."

13. Sinkovich, "Police Search Car."

14. Sinkovich, "2 Jailed."

15. Sinkovich, "Charge of Gun Theft."

16. Sinkovich, "Letters Revealed."

17. Sinkovich, "2 Jailed."

18. Peggy Sinkovich, "Jury Issues Indictment of Premeditated Murder," *Youngstown (Ohio) Vindicator,* December 29, 2001.

19. See Amanda C. Davis, "Jury Issues Indictment of Premeditated Murder; The Two Will Be Arraigned Monday in the Death of Robert Fingerhut," *Youngstown (Ohio) Vindicator,* December 29, 2001.

20. Sinkovich, "Jury Issues."

21. Sinkovich, "Letters Reveal."

22. Sinkovich, "2 Jailed."

23. Sinkovich, "Letters Reveal."

24. Sinkovich, "Lawyers Want Statement."

25. Peggy Sinkovich, "Videotape Won't Be Used in Murder Trial," *Youngstown (Ohio) Vindicator,* July 19, 2002.

26. Sinkovich, "Lawyers Want Statement."

27. Peggy Sinkovich, "Trial Begins in Howland Killing," *Youngstown (Ohio) Vindicator,* October 8, 2002.

28. Sinkovich, "Lawyers Want Statement."

29. Ibid.

30. Sinkovich, "Videotape."

31. Peggy Sinkovich, "Murder Trial Gets under Way," *Youngstown (Ohio) Vindicator,* October 24, 2002.

32. Peggy Sinkovich, "Jury Deliberates Murder Case," *Youngstown (Ohio) Vindicator,* November 7, 2002.

33. Peter H. Milliken, "Jury Finds Man Guilty in Slaying," *Youngstown (Ohio) Vindicator,* November 9, 2002.

34. Peggy Sinkovich, "Defense to Recall Killer's Childhood," *Youngstown (Ohio) Vindicator,* November 12, 2002.

35. Peggy Sinkovich, "Hearing Set on Killer's Penalty," *Youngstown (Ohio) Vindicator,* November 21, 2002.

36. Peggy Sinkovich, "Jurors Mull Death Sentence," *Youngstown (Ohio) Vindicator,* November 15, 2002.

37. Peggy Sinkovich, "Judge to Mull Death Penalty for Jackson," *Youngstown (Ohio) Vindicator,* November 27, 2002.

38. Peggy Sinkovich, "Jury Recommends Death in Murder Case," *Youngstown (Ohio) Vindicator,* November 16, 2002.

39. Peggy Sinkovich, "Capital Murder Jury Is Still Being Seated," *Youngstown (Ohio) Vindicator,* May 4, 2003.

40. Peggy Sinkovich, "Defense Asks to Move Murder Trial," *Youngstown (Ohio) Vindicator,* April 12, 2003.

41. Peggy Sinkovich, "Murder Trial Jurors Chosen," *Youngstown (Ohio) Vindicator,* May 16, 2003.

42. Peggy Sinkovich, "Roberts Makes Opening," *Youngstown (Ohio) Vindicator,* May 17, 2003.

43. Peggy Sinkovich, "Howland Woman Awaits Verdict in Murder," *Youngstown (Ohio) Vindicator,* May 31, 2003.

44. Peggy Sinkovich, "Jury Recommends Death Sentence," *Youngstown (Ohio) Vindicator,* June 8, 2003.

45. "Ohio Woman Gets Death Sentence," *Cleveland Plain Dealer,* June 22, 2003; Sinkovich, "Roberts' Lawyers Consider Appeal."

46. Sinkovich, "Jury Recommends."

47. "State Is Ready for What Could Be First Woman on Death Row Since '91," *Lima (Ohio) News,* June 10, 2003.

48. "Will Roberts End up on Death Row?," *Youngstown (Ohio) Vindicator,* June 13, 2003. See Victor L. Streib, "Death Penalty for Female Offenders" (quarterly Web report), http://www.law.onu.edu/faculty/streib/streib.htm.

49. State of Ohio v. Donna Roberts, Case Number 03–1441, Supreme Court of Ohio.

50. Merit Brief of Appellant, Donna Roberts, State of Ohio v. Donna Roberts, Case Number 03–1441 (filed July 19, 2004), 4.

51. Ibid., 8–13.

52. Ibid., 29–30.

53. Ibid., 41–42.

54. Sinkovich, "Jury Recommends."

55. Merit Brief of Appellant, 18–24.

56. Ibid., 36–40.

57. Ibid., 59–92.

58. Ibid., 60.

59. Merit Brief Plaintiff-Appellee of State of Ohio, State of Ohio v. Donna Roberts, Case Number 03–1441 (filed November 1, 2004), 40.

60. "Only Female Death Row Inmate Describes Poor Conditions," *Lima (Ohio) News,* November 2, 2003.

61. Sinkovich, "Videotape."

62. Sinkovich, "2 Jailed."

63. Sinkovich, "Lawyers Want Statement."

64. Sinkovich, "Roberts Makes Opening."

65. Sinkovich, "Jury Recommends."

66. Sinkovich, "Roberts' Lawyers."

67. Sinkovich, "2 Jailed."

68. Sinkovich, "Letters Reveal."

Chapter 20

1. Alex M. Parker, "Diar Gets Death," *Lorain (Ohio) Morning Journal,* November 3, 2005.

2. Scot Allyn, "Death Row: Few Visits with No Contact, Little Rec Time," *Lorain (Ohio) Morning Journal,* November 5, 2005.

3. Scot Allyn, "Attorney Working to Build Diar Legal Team," *Lorain (Ohio) Morning Journal,* November 5, 2005.

4. Mark Puente, "Mom Convicted in 4-Year-Old's Home Fire Death," *Cleveland Plain Dealer,* October 18, 2005; Mark Puente, "Mother Sobs before Getting Death Sentence," *Cleveland Plain Dealer,* November 3, 2005.

5. Rachel Dissell, "Mom Burned as a Child Loses Her Son to Flames," *Cleveland Plain Dealer,* August 28, 2003.

6. Rachel Dissell, "Fiery Death of Child Linked to Painful Blaze 25 Years Ago; Mom Accused of Killing Son Was Disfigured When She Was 4," *Cleveland Plain Dealer,* May 16, 2004.

7. Chris O'Connell, "Mother Testifies in Defense of Daughter Accused of Killing Toddler," Court TV, October 14, 2005.

8. Dissell, "Fiery Death."

9. Rachel Dissell, "Lorain Woman Killed Son, 4, and Set Fire, Prosecutors Say," *Cleveland Plain Dealer,* May 4, 2004; Chris O'Connell, "Coroner: Child Had Been Killed before Flames Burned His House," Court TV, October 5, 2005.

10. Chris O'Connell, "In Police Interview, Mother Suggests 4-Year-Old Might Have Started Fatal Fire," Court TV, October 7, 2005; O'Connell, "Mother Testifies."

11. Dissell, "Fiery Death."

12. Puente, "Mother Sobs."

13. Dissell, "Mom Burned"; Mike Sakal, "Former Home of Nicole Diar May Be Going on Market," *Lorain (Ohio) Morning Journal,* November 17, 2005.

14. Rachel Dissell, "Boy in Lorain House Fire Was Intentionally Killed," *Cleveland Plain Dealer,* October 7, 2003.

15. Dissell, "Fiery Death."

16. O'Connell, "Coroner."

17. Puente, "Mom Convicted."

18. Docket sheet, State of Ohio v. Nicole Diar, Case Number 04CR065248, Lorain County Court of Common Pleas, Elyria, Ohio (accessed on November 9, 2005), 1; Dissell, "Lorain Woman."

19. Dissell, "Lorain Woman."

20. See, e.g., Dissell, "Lorain Woman"; Dissell, "Fiery Death."

21. Docket sheet, 4; "Law and Order: Prosecutors Want Case Kept Quiet," *Cleveland Plain Dealer,* May 26, 2004.

22. Docket sheet, 6; Rachel Dissell, "Judge Won't Issue Gag Order in Toddler-Death Case, For Now," *Cleveland Plain Dealer,* June 10, 2004.

23. Docket sheet, 2–11.

24. Ibid., 7.

25. Ibid., 1; Mark Puente, "Burn Victim Faces Trial in Son's Fiery Death," *Cleveland Plain Dealer,* September 26, 2005.

26. Docket sheet, 11; Puente, "Mom Convicted"; Mark Puente, "Mom on Trial in Slaying of Son, 4," *Cleveland Plain Dealer,* October 4, 2005.

27. Puente, "Burn Victim." See, e.g., Chris O'Connell, "Prosecutor Says Woman Killed Her Own Toddler out of Selfishness," Court TV, October 4, 2005; Bo Rosser, "Ohio Mother Receives Death Sentence for Killing Her Toddler," Court TV, November 2, 2005.

28. Puente, "Mom on Trial"; O'Connell, "Prosecutor Says."

29. O'Connell, "Coroner."

30. Ibid.; O'Connell, "Prosecutor Says."

31. Puente, "Mom on Trial."

32. Mark Puente, "After Burying Son, Mom Sang and Danced at Bar," *Cleveland Plain Dealer,* October 14, 2005.

33. Chris O'Connell, "Pastor: Woman Accused of Slaying Her Son Feared Being Murdered," Court TV, October 15, 2005.

34. O'Connell, "Prosecutor Says"; Puente, "Mom on Trial."

35. O'Connell, "Coroner"; Chris O'Connell, "Jury Gets Case of Mother Accused of Slaying Son, Setting Home on Fire," Court TV, October 17, 2005.

36. O'Connell, "Jury Gets Case."

37. O'Connell, "Mother Testifies"; O'Connell, "Pastor."

38. Puente, "After Burying Son."

39. Docket sheet, 14; Puente, "Mom Convicted."

40. Alex M. Parker, "Diar Convicted: Jury Delivers Verdict in Less Than Four Hours," *Lorain (Ohio) Morning Journal,* October 18, 2005.

41. "Jurors: Evidence Clear in Mother's Death-Penalty Case," *Lima (Ohio) News,* November 4, 2005.

42. "Docket," 15.

43. Mark Puente, "Jury Deliberates Diar's Sentence," *Cleveland Plain Dealer,* November 2, 2005; Bo Rosser, "Jurors Weigh Death Penalty for Mother Convicted of Killing Her 4-Year-Old Son," Court TV, November 1, 1005.

44. Puente, "Jury Deliberates."

45. "Docket," 15.

46. Parker, "Diar Gets Death."

47. Puente, "Mother Sobs."

48. "Jurors: Evidence Clear."

49. Puente, "Mother Sobs"; Allyn, "Death Row: Few Visits."

50. Allyn, "Attorney Working."

51. Sakal, "Former Home."

52. Allyn, "Death Row: Few Visits."

Chapter 21

1. Alfred Emory Lee, *History of the City of Columbus, Capital of Ohio* (New York: Munsell, 1892), 2:581; "A Woman Condemned to Be Hung in Ohio," *Raleigh Register and North Carolina Gazette,* January 12, 1844; "West End Woman Strangled, Drowned in Sharon Woods," *Cincinnati Enquirer,* September 7, 1952.

2. Lee, *History of the City,* 2:581; "West End Woman."

3. Ibid; Elizabeth Rapaport, "Some Questions about Gender and the Death Penalty," *Golden Gate University Law Review* 20 (Fall 1990): 525.

4. Lee, *History of the City,* 2:581.

5. "West End Woman."

6. Lee, *History of the City,* 2:581.

7. "Rival Choked and Drowned, Woman Held for Grand Jury," *Cincinnati Enquirer,* September 8, 1952.

8. "Woman Condemned."

9. "West End Woman."

10. "3d Woman Pays with Life in Ohio's Electric Chair," *Cleveland Plain Dealer,* June 12, 1954.

11. See Victor L. Streib, "Death Penalty for Battered Women," *Florida State Law Review* 20 (Summer 1992): 163–94.

12. See Wayne R. LaFave, *Principles of Criminal Law* (St. Paul, Minn.: Thomson West, 2003), 598.

13. See Coker v. Georgia, 433 U.S. 584 (1977); and Victor L. Streib, *Death Penalty in a Nutshell,* 2d ed. (St. Paul, Minn.: Thomson West, 2005), 65–68.

14. "Rival Choked"; "West End Woman."

15. "West End Woman"; "3d Woman."

16. "Prosecution Files Brief in Dean Case," *Batavia (Ohio) Clermont Courier,* April 9, 1953.

17. "Death Chair Seals Lips of Blond Slayer; Events of Early Life to Remain a Mystery," *Cincinnati Enquirer,* December 8, 1938.

18. Kerry Segrave, *Women Serial and Mass Murderers: A Worldwide Reference, 1580 through 1990* (Jefferson, N.C.: McFarland, 1993), 162; "Defense Fights Murder Confession," *Batavia (Ohio) Clermont Sun,* December 11, 1952; "Lies, All Lies Anna Hahn Exclaims under State Grilling in Murder Case," *Cincinnati Enquirer,* November 2, 1937.

19. "Fight to Save Mrs. Dean from Chair," *Batavia (Ohio) Clermont Sun,* December 18, 1952.

20. "Poison Murder Trial to Begin Dec. 8," *Batavia (Ohio) Clermont Sun,* November 20, 1952.

21. "Mrs. Dean Faces Murder Charge, *Batavia (Ohio) Clermont Sun,* September 18, 1952; "Wagner's Physician Testifies in Hahn Case," *Cincinnati Enquirer,* October 16, 1937.

22. "Authorities Pursue Poison Probe," *Batavia (Ohio) Clermont Sun,* September 11, 1952.

23. "Trial Marks Anna Hahn, *Cincinnati Enquirer,* October 23, 1937.

24. "Fight to Save."

25. "Mrs. Dean Unemotional as Murder Trial Opens," *Clermont Courier* (Batavia, Ohio), December 11, 1952.

26. "Death Chair."

27. "Arsenic Poisoning Reported," *Clermont Courier* (Batavia, Ohio), August 28, 1952.

28. "Seven Jurors Chosen in Hahn Murder Trial; Death Penalty Hinted," *Cincinnati Enquirer,* October 12, 1937.

29. "Authorities Pursue."

30. "Trial Marks"; "Interview Is Off, Then Mrs. Hahn Relents," *Cincinnati Enquirer,* August 18, 1937.

31. See chapter 5, table 5.1.

32. Ibid.

33. "Defense Fights."

34. "West End Woman"; "3d Woman."

35. "Fight to Save."

36. "Rival Choked."

37. "Betty Butler Dies"; "Electric Chair."

Chapter 22

1. Randall M. Dana, "Background Information Provided," January 10, 1991 (press release from Public Defender of the State of Ohio, copy on file with author).

2. Peggy Sinkovich, "2 Jailed, Charged in Man's Slaying," *Youngstown (Ohio) Vindicator,* December 21, 2001.

3. State v. Osborne, 49 Ohio St. 2d 135, 138, 359 N.E.2d 78, 81 (1976); "Two Women Found Beaten to Death in Ottawa Hills Home," *Toledo Blade,* November 20, 1975.

4. State v. Young, No. C-870394, 1988 WL 85903, *1 (Ohio Ct. App. 1st Dist. Aug. 17 1988).

5. Peggy Sinkovich, "Jury Recommends Death Sentence," *Youngstown (Ohio) Vindicator,* June 8, 2003.

6. Dana, "Background Information."

7. Atkins v. Virginia, 536 U.S. 304 (2002).

8. State v. Lockett, 49 Ohio St. 2d 48, 51, 358 N.E.2d 1062, 1066 (1976).

9. State v. Young, No, C-830757, 1986 WL 5503, *3 (Ohio Ct. App. 1st Dist. May 14, 1986).

10. Dana, "Background Information."

11. See chapter 4.

12. Mary Beth Lane, "Celeste Commutes Eight Death Sentences," *Cleveland Plain Dealer,* January 11, 1991.

13. Tison v. Arizona, 481 U.S. 137, 158 (1987); Enmund v. Florida, 458 U.S. 782, 801 (1982).

14. See Victor L. Streib, "Death Penalty for Female Offenders," July 1, 2005, 15–20 (quarterly Web report), http://www.law.onu.edu/faculty/streib/streib.htm.

Conclusion

1. See chapters 1 and 2.

2. See table 5.1 and chapter 5.

3. See chapters 3 and 4.

4. See Victor L. Streib, "Capital Punishment of Children in Ohio: 'They'd Never Send a Boy of Seventeen to the Chair in Ohio, Would They?,'" *Akron Law Review* 18 (Summer 1984): 51–102.

5. See chapter 6.

6. See chapter 7.

7. See chapter 8.

8. See chapter 9.

9. See Victor L. Streib, "Death Penalty for Female Offenders" (quarterly Web report), http://www.law.onu.edu/faculty/streib/streib.htm.

10. See chapters 19 and 20.

11. Streib, "Death Penalty for Female Offenders," October 3, 2005, 6 (quarterly Web report), http://www.law.onu.edu/faculty/streib/streib.htm.

BIBLIOGRAPHY

Cases

Atkins v. Virginia, 536 U.S. 304 (2002)

Coker v. Georgia, 433 U.S. 584 (1977)

Cooper v. State, 540 N.E.2d 1216 (Ind. 1989)

Eddings v. Oklahoma, 455 U.S. 104 (1982)

Enmund v. Florida, 458 U.S. 782 (1982)

Furman v. Georgia, 408 U.S. 238 (1972)

Gregg v. Georgia, 428 U.S. 153 (1976)

Lockett v. Ohio, 438 U.S. 586 (1978)

Ohio v. Brown, 489 U.S. 1040 (1989)

Ohio v. Green, 510 U.S. 891 (1993)

Poole v. Perini, 659 F.2d 730 (6th Cir. 1981), *cert. denied*, 455 U.S. 910 (1982)

State ex rel. Brown v. Dana, 66 Ohio App. 3d 709, 586 N.E.2d 150 (1990)

State of Ohio v. Donna Roberts, Case Number 03–1441, Supreme Court of Ohio

State of Ohio v. Nicole Diar. Case Number 04CR065248, Lorain County Court of Common Pleas, Elyria, Ohio

State v. Brown, 38 Ohio St. 3d 305, 528 N.E.2d 523 (1988)

State v. Brown, 39 Ohio St. 3d 717, 534 N.E.2d 93 (1988)

State v. Brown, No. C-850 434, 1987 WL 9743 (Ohio Ct. App. 1st Dist. April 15, 1987)

State v. Dean, 94 Ohio App. 540, 116 N.E.2d 767 (1953)

State v. Grant, 67 Ohio St. 3d 465, 620 N.E.2d 50 (1993)

State v. Grant, 68 Ohio St. 3d 1412, 623 N.E.2d 568 (1993)

State v. Grant, No. 83 C.A. 144, 1990 Ohio App. LEXIS 4949 (7th Dist. Nov. 9, 1990)

State v. Green, 66 Ohio St. 3d 141, 609 N.E.2d 1253 (1993)

State v. Green, No. C-880 504, 1990 Ohio App. LEXIS 2798 (July 11, 1990)

State v. Hahn, 10 Ohio Op. 29 (1937)

State v. Hahn, 59 Ohio App. 178, 17 N.E.2d 392 (1938)

State v. Lampkin, No. C-890273, 1990 Ohio App. LEXIS 4315 (1st Dist. Oct. 3, 1990)

State v. Leigh, 31 Ohio St. 2d 97, 285 N.E.2d 333 (1972)

State v. Lockett, 49 Ohio St. 2d 48, 358 N.E.2d 1062 (1976)

State v. Osborne, 49 Ohio St. 2d 135, 359 N.E.2d 78 (1976)

State v. Smith, No. L-77–277 (Ohio Ct. App. 6th Dist. Feb. 16, 1979)

State v. Wernert, C.A. No. L-76–327, 1979 Ohio App. LEXIS 9325 (May 25, 1979)

State v. Wernert, No. CR 75–7249, 1984 WL 14306 (Ohio Ct. App. 6th Dist. Oct. 19, 1984)

State v. Wernert, No. CR 75–7249B, 1982 WL 6371 (Ohio Ct. App. 6th Dist. Apr. 23, 1982)

State v. Young, No. C-830757, 1986 WL 5503 (Ohio Ct. App. 1st Dist. May 14, 1986)

State v. Young, No. C-870394, 1988 WL 85903 (Ohio Ct. App. 1st Dist. Aug. 17, 1988)

Tison v. Arizona, 481 U.S. 137 (1987)

Wernert v. Arn, 484 U.S. 1011 (1988)

Wernert v. Arn, 819 F.2d 613 (6th Cir. 1987)

Wernert v. Ohio, 446 U.S. 942 (1980)

Wernert v. Wernert, 61 Ohio Misc. 2d 436 (Ohio Com. Pl. 1991)

Wilkinson v. Maurer, No. 91CVH-01–763, slip op., 12 (Franklin County Ct. Com. Pl. February 13, 1992)

Wilkinson v. Maurer, No. 92AP-674, slip op., 30 (Ohio Ct. App. 10th Dist. April 8, 1993)

Books, Periodicals, and Other Publications

"Accused Kin Is Beneficiary under 2 Wills." *Toledo Blade,* December 1, 1975.

"All Doubt of Blonde's Guilt Dissipated by Confession Penned in Prison Cell." *Cincinnati Enquirer,* December 19, 1938.

Allyn, Scot. "Attorney Working to Build Diar Legal Team." *Lorain (Ohio) Morning Journal,* November 5, 2005.

———. "Death Row: Few Visits with No Contact, Little Rec Time." *Lorain (Ohio) Morning Journal,* November 5, 2005.

Anderson, John. "The Movies Seldom Combine Real Life with Death Penalty Situations; Dramatic Tension and Pathos, Not the Justice of State-Sponsored

Executions, Are the Stuff of Most Films on the Subject." *Los Angeles Times,* March 17, 2003.

"Anna Hahn Arrived in City on Uncle's $236, Not $16,000." *Cincinnati Enquirer,* August 17, 1937.

"Anna Hahn Either Innocent or Insane, Attorney Avers in Final Appeal for Mercy." *Cincinnati Enquirer,* December 2, 1938.

"Anna Hahn Falls and Is Carried to Chair; Dies after She Cries Appeal to Spectators." *Cincinnati Enquirer,* December 8, 1938.

"Anna Hahn on Stand in Own Defense; Son Is also to Testify." *Cincinnati Enquirer,* November 1, 1937.

"Anna Hahn's Death Cell Confession! Four Cincinnati Murders Are Laid Bare." *Cincinnati Enquirer,* December 19, 1938.

"Anna Hahn's Fate in Jury's Hands." *Cincinnati Enquirer,* November 6, 1937.

"Anna Hahn's Trial Halted Temporarily over Question of Embalming Powder." *Cincinnati Enquirer* October 21, 1937.

"Anna Hahn to Die Tonight." *Cincinnati Enquirer,* December 7, 1938.

"Appeals Could Delay Execution of Pair under Death Sentence." *Toledo Blade,* December 1, 1977.

"Appeals Court Reviewing Details of Dean Case." *Batavia (Ohio) Clermont Courier,* April 13, 1953.

"Arsenic Poisoning Reported." *Batavia (Ohio) Clermont Courier,* August 28, 1952.

"Arterberry Denies Killing Pair, Calls Confession to Police a Lie." *Toledo Blade,* September 18, 1976.

"Attorney asks for New Trial." *Cincinnati Enquirer,* November 9, 1937.

Atwood, Jane Evelyn. *Too Much Time: Women in Prison.* Paris: Phaidon, 2000.

"Authorities Pursue Poison Probe." *Batavia (Ohio) Clermont Sun,* September 11, 1952.

Ballinger, Anette. *Dead Woman Walking: Executed Women in England and Wales 1900–1955.* Aldershot, England: Ashgate, 2000.

Banner, Stuart. *The Death Penalty, An American History.* Cambridge: Harvard University Press, 2002.

"Benita Smith Role in Vinnedge Case Called a Major One." *Toledo Blade,* September 1, 1977.

Benson, David J. "Constitutionality of Ohio's New Death Penalty Statute." *University of Toledo Law Review* 14 (Fall 1982): 77–97.

Berger, Raul. *Death Penalties: The Supreme Court's Obstacle Course.* Cambridge: Harvard University Press, 1982.

"Betty Butler Dies." *Cincinnati Enquirer,* June 12, 1954.

Bowers, William J. *Legal Homicide: Death as Punishment in America, 1864–1982.* Boston: Northeastern University Press, 1984.

"Britain Retains Death Penalty Ban." *Toledo Blade,* December 12, 1975.

Broomfield, Nick. *Aileen Wuornos: The Selling of a Serial Killer* (1992), http://www.nickbroomfield.com/aileenwuornos.html.

Broomfield, Nick, and Joan Churchill. *Aileen: Life and Death of a Serial Killer* (2004), http://www.aileenfilm.com.

Brown, Geoff. "Penn Portrait Shaded with a Heavy Hand." *Times* (London), August 15, 1996.

Brown, Wenzell. *Women Who Died in the Chair.* New York: Collier, 1958.

Carroll, Jenny E. "Images of Women and Capital Sentencing among Female Offenders: Exploring the Outer Limits of the Eighth Amendment and Articulated Theories of Justice." *Texas Law Review* 75 (May 1997): 1413–53.

"Child Slayer Sentenced to Die." *Youngstown (Ohio) Vindicator,* October 22, 1983.

"Clemency Hearing for Mrs. Dean Set." *Batavia (Ohio) Clermont Courier,* October 15, 1953.

"Clemency Hearing to Decide Fate of Dovie Dean." *Batavia (Ohio) Clermont Courier,* October 29, 1953.

"Closing Arguments Today." *Cincinnati Enquirer,* November 4, 1937.

"Commuted Death Sentences Fought in Ohio." *New York Times,* January 30, 1991.

"Couple Enter Innocent Pleas to Charges of Murdering Kin." *Toledo Blade,* December 31, 1975.

"Court Affirms Murder Verdict." *Batavia (Ohio) Clermont Courier,* May 21, 1953.

Crocker, Phyllis L. "Is the Death Penalty Good for Women?" *Buffalo Criminal Law Review* 4, no.2 (2001): 917–65.

Dana, Randall M. "Background Information Provided." January 10, 1991 (press release from Public Defender for the State of Ohio, copy on file with author).

Davis, Amanda C. "Jury Issues Indictment of Premeditated Murder; The Two Will Be Arraigned Monday in the Death of Robert Fingerhut." *Youngstown (Ohio) Vindicator,* December 29, 2001.

"Dean Case Taken to First District Court of Appeals." *Batavia (Ohio) Clermont Courier,* March 26, 1953.

"Dean Verdict Appealed." *Batavia (Ohio) Clermont Courier,* December 18, 1952.

"Death Chair Seals Lips of Blond Slayer; Events of Early Life to Remain a Mystery." *Cincinnati Enquirer,* December 8, 1938.

"Death Penalty Hearing Scheduled November 22 for Wernerts, Arterberry." *Toledo Blade,* September 22, 1976.

Death Penalty Information Center. Washington, D.C. http://www.deathpenaltyinfo
.org.

"Death Penalty Residents." Public Defender's Office. May–July 1991 (State Defender's Report).

"Death Possible for Miss Grant." *Youngstown (Ohio) Vindicator,* October 14, 1983.

"Defense Fights Murder Confession." *Batavia (Ohio) Clermont Sun,* December 11, 1952.

"Defense Rests in Theodore Smith Murder Trial, Prosecution Continues Evidence against Sister." *Toledo Blade,* September 8, 1977.

Dennis, Debra. "Woman Who Broke Ohio Death Penalty Faces Prison Again." *Cleveland Plain Dealer,* March 5, 1997.

"Dispute Delays Hahn Trial, Scope of Evidence Argued." *Cincinnati Enquirer,* October 22, 1937.

Dissell, Rachel. "Boy in Lorain House Fire Was Intentionally Killed." *Cleveland Plain Dealer,* October 7, 2003.

———. "Fiery Death of Child Linked to Painful Blaze 25 Years Ago; Mom Accused of Killing Son Was Disfigured When She Was 4." *Cleveland Plain Dealer,* May 16, 2004.

———. "Judge Won't Issue Gag Order in Toddler-Death Case, For Now." *Cleveland Plain Dealer,* June 10, 2004.

———. "Lorain Woman Killed Son, 4, and Set Fire, Prosecutors Say." *Cleveland Plain Dealer,* May 4, 2004.

———. "Mom Burned as a Child Loses Her Son to Flames." *Cleveland Plain Dealer,* August 28, 2003.

"Dovie Dean to Die June 5 in Electric Chair." *Batavia (Ohio) Clermont Courier,* February 26, 1953.

Eckhoff, Jeff. "Jury Calls for Johnson's Death." *Des Moines (Iowa) Register,* June 22, 2005.

"8 Death Sentences Commuted in Ohio." *New York Times,* January 12, 1991.

"Electric Chair Fails to Disturb Dovie Dean's Perfect Emotional Control in Last Moments." *Batavia (Ohio) Clermont Courier,* January 21, 1954.

Espy, Watt. "List of Confirmations, State-by-State, of Legal Executions as of August 10, 1998." Unpublished report, Capital Punishment Research Project, Headland, Alabama, August 1998.

"The Execution." *Cleveland Plain Dealer,* February 14, 1844.

"Execution Date Set." *Batavia (Ohio) Clermont Courier,* October 8, 1953.

"Eyewitness Account of Dean Execution." *Batavia (Ohio) Clermont Courier,* January 21, 1954.

"Fight to Save Mrs. Dean from Chair." *Batavia (Ohio) Clermont Sun,* December 18, 1952.

Fletcher, Beverly R., Lynda Dixon Shaver, and Dreama G. Moon, eds. *Women Prisoners: A Forgotten Population.* Westport, Conn.: Praeger, 1993.

Fogle, H. M. *The Palace of Death; or, the Ohio Penitentiary Annex.* Columbus, Ohio: privately printed, 1908.

"Funerals Held for Gray, Mrs. Snyder." *New York Daily News,* January 14, 1928.

Geiger, Anthony L., and Scott Selbach. "S.B. 1: Ohio Enacts Death Penalty Statute." *University of Dayton Law Review* 7 (Spring 1982): 531–66.

Gillespie, L. Kay. *Dancehall Ladies: Executed Women of the 20th Century.* Lanham, Md.: University Press of America, 2000.

"Given Reprieve by Governor Lausche." *Batavia (Ohio) Clermont Courier,* November 5, 1953.

Guttenberg, Jack A. "Recent Changes in Ohio Sentencing Law: The Questions Left Unanswered." *University of Toledo Law Review* 15 (Fall 1983): 35–69.

"Hahn Death Set for December 7." *Cincinnati Enquirer,* November 17, 1938.

"Hahn Jury Completed; Eleven Women Chosen; Hearing Begins Today." *Cincinnati Enquirer,* October 15, 1937.

"Hahn Letters." *Cincinnati Enquirer,* December 14, 1938.

"Hahn Letters in Safe at Home for Several Days, Hoodin Says; Boy's Care in Attorneys' Hands." *Cincinnati Enquirer,* December 9, 1938.

"Hahn Plea Put before Davey." *Cincinnati Enquirer,* November 18, 1938.

"Hahn Trial Is to Open Today." *Cincinnati Enquirer,* October 11, 1937.

Haller, Kathryn. "Capital Punishment Statutes after Furman." *Ohio State Law Journal* 35, no. 3 (1974): 651–85.

Hanna, Janan. "Alton Coleman Ally Sought by Indiana." *Chicago Tribune,* January 12, 1991.

Harding, Roberta M. "Celluloid Death: Cinematic Depictions of Capital Punishment." *University of San Francisco Law Review* 30 (Summer 1996): 1167–79.

Hart, William H. "Capital Punishment in Ohio: The Constitutionality of the Death Penalty Statute." *University of Dayton Law Review* 3 (Winter 1978): 169–96.

Heintz, Jeffrey T. "Legislative Response to Furman v. Georgia—Ohio Restores the Death Penalty." *Akron Law Review* 8 (Fall 1974): 149–61.

Hilliard, Elaine C. "Capital Punishment in Ohio: Aggravating Circumstances." *Cleveland State Law Review* 31, no. 3 (1982): 495–528.

"History of the Death Penalty in Ohio." http://www.ohiodeathrow.com.

Hood, Roger. *The Death Penalty: A World-Wide Perspective.* Rev. ed. Oxford: Clarendon, 1996.

Howarth, Joan W. "Deciding to Kill: Revealing the Gender in the Task Handed to Capital Jurors." *Wisconsin Law Review* 1994, no. 6:1345–1424.

———. "Executing White Masculinities: Learning from Karla Faye Tucker." *Oregon Law Review* 81 (Spring 2002): 183–229.

———. "Feminism, Lawyering, and Death Row." *Southern California Review of Law and Women's Studies* 2 (Fall 1992): 401–25.

"Interview Is Off, Then Mrs. Hahn Relents." *Cincinnati Enquirer,* August 18, 1937.

Johnson, Paula C. *Inner Lives: Voices of African American Women in Prison.* New York: New York University Press, 2003.

Jones, Ann. *Women Who Kill.* New York: Fawcett Columbine, 1980.

"Judge Voids Clemency for Eleven Prisoners." *Cleveland Plain Dealer,* February 14, 1992.

"Judge's Ruling Awaited on Dean New Trial Motion." *Batavia (Ohio) Clermont Courier,* January 11, 1953.

"Jurors: Evidence Clear in Mother's Death-Penalty Case." *Lima (Ohio) News,* November 4, 2005.

"Jurors in Benita Smith's Trial Slated to Begin Deliberations." *Toledo Blade,* September 10, 1977.

"Jury Deciding If Miss Grant Is Guilty in Deaths of Her Two Children." *Youngstown (Ohio) Vindicator,* October 13, 1983.

"Jury Deliberations Begin in Trials of 3 in Wernerts Case." *Toledo Blade,* September 20, 1976.

"Jury Selection Starts in Vinnedge Case." *Toledo Blade,* August 29, 1977.

"Jury Told Vinnedge Murder Suspect Burned Lamson's Bag." *Toledo Blade,* September 2, 1977.

Kaplan, David A., and Nadine Joseph. "'Live, From San Quentin . . . .'" *Newsweek,* April 1, 1991, 61.

Kawa, Barry. "2 Sides to Argue 7 Killers' Fates." *Cleveland Plain Dealer,* September 19, 1994.

King, Rachel, and Judy Bellin. *The Forgotten Population: A Look at Death Row in the United States Through the Experiences of Women.* New York: American Civil Liberties Union and American Friends Service Committee, December 2004.

Kopec, Janice L. "Avoiding a Death Sentence in the American Legal System: Get a Woman to Do It." *Capital Defense Journal* 15 (Spring 2003): 353–82.

Kuncl, Tom. *Death Row Women.* New York: Pocket Books, 1994.

Kuncl, Tom, and Paul Einstein. *Ladies Who Kill.* New York: Pinnacle Books, 1985.

Kuzma, Susan M. "The Constitutionality of Ohio's Death Penalty." *Ohio State Law Journal* 38, no. 3 (1977): 617–75.

LaFave, Wayne R. *Principles of Criminal Law.* St. Paul, Minn.: Thomson West, 2003.

Lane, Mary Beth. "Celeste Commutes Eight Death Sentences." *Cleveland Plain Dealer,* January 11, 1991.

Last Dance. Touchstone Pictures and Buena Vista Pictures. 1996.

Laurence, John. *The History of Capital Punishment.* Secaucus, N.J.: Citadel, 1960.

"Law and Order: Prosecutors Want Case Kept Quiet." *Cleveland Plain Dealer,* May 26, 2004.

Laws Passed in the Territory of the United States North-West of the River Ohio. Philadelphia: Printed by F. Childs and J. Swaine, 1788. Microfiche, Buffalo, N.Y.: Hein, 1986.

Lee, Alfred Emery. *History of the City of Columbus, Capital of Ohio.* New York: Munsell, 1892.

"Lies, All Lies Anna Hahn Exclaims under State Grilling in Murder Case." *Cincinnati Enquirer,* November 2, 1937.

Lore, David. "The Pen." *Columbus Dispatch Magazine,* October 28, 1984, 10.

"March 10 Set as Death Date for Blond German Slayer; Anna Hahn Faints in Cell." *Cincinnati Enquirer,* November 28, 1937.

Maslin, Janet. "Death Row Diva: A Raw Sharon Stone." *New York Times,* May 3, 1996.

Milliken, Peter H. "Jury Finds Man Guilty in Slaying." *Youngstown (Ohio) Vindicator,* November 9, 2002.

Mintz, Morton. "Three Major Court Rulings; Imposing Death Penalty Made Harder." *Washington Post,* July 4, 1978.

"Mrs. Dean Faces Murder Charge." *Batavia (Ohio) Clermont Sun,* September 18, 1952.

"Mrs. Dean Not Now Sane, Defense Attorneys Claim; Trial Is Delayed." *Batavia (Ohio) Clermont Sun,* October 9, 1952.

"Mrs. Dean Ruled Sane by Common Pleas Court." *Batavia (Ohio) Clermont Courier,* November 20, 1952.

"Mrs. Dean's Murder Trial Rescheduled." *Batavia (Ohio) Clermont Courier,* November 13, 1952.

"Mrs. Dean's Murder Trial to Begin October 20; Will Cost County $4,000." *Batavia (Ohio) Clermont Sun,* September 25, 1952.

"Mrs. Dean Unemotional as Murder Trial Opens." *Batavia (Ohio) Clermont Courier,* December 11, 1952.

"Murder Jury Is Still Incomplete; Ten Women in Tentative Panel after Night Session of Hahn Trial." *Cincinnati Enquirer,* October 14, 1937.

"Murders of Ottawa Hills Women Intended as Mercy Killings, Tape Played at Trial Says." *Toledo Blade,* September 15, 1976.

"Murder Trial Begins Monday." *Batavia (Ohio) Clermont Sun,* December 4, 1952.

"Murder Trial Date Set for Mrs. Dovie Dean Is Oct. 20." *Batavia (Ohio) Clermont Courier,* September 25, 1952.

NAACP Legal Defense and Education Fund, Inc. "Death Row USA" (quarterly report listing all executions, all prisoners on death row, and other pertinent information concerning current death row practices), Summer 2005.

Nash, Jay Robert. *Look for the Woman: A Narrative Encyclopedia of Female Poisoners, Kidnappers, Thieves, Terrorists, Swindlers and Spies from Elizabethan Times to the Present.* London: Harrap Publishers, 1984.

O'Connell, Chris. "Coroner: Child Had Been Killed before Flames Burned His House." Court TV, October 5, 2005.

———. "In Police Interview, Mother Suggests 4-Year-Old Might Have Started Fatal Fire." Court TV, October 7, 2005.

———. "Jury Gets Case of Mother Accused of Slaying Son, Setting Home on Fire." Court TV, October 17, 2005.

———. "Mother Testifies in Defense of Daughter Accused of Killing Toddler." Court TV, October 14, 2005.

———. "Pastor: Woman Accused of Slaying Her Son Feared Being Murdered." Court TV, October 15, 2005.

———. "Prosecutor Says Woman Killed Her Own Toddler out of Selfishness." Court TV, October 4, 2005.

O'Donnell, Bernard. *Should Women Hang?* London: W. H. Allen, 1956.

Office of the Attorney General of Ohio. "Capital Crimes Annual Report; 2003 Update—State and Federal Cases." http://www.ag.state.oh.us/online_publications/capital_crimes/annual_report_capital_crimes_2004.pdf (April 1, 2004).

"Officials Probe Death of Farmer." *Batavia (Ohio) Clermont Courier,* September 4, 1952.

Ohio Department of Rehabilitation and Correction. "Capital Punishment in Ohio." http://www.drc.state.oh.us/public/capital.htm.

———. "Offender Data, Beatrice Lampkin—W 025931" (Offender Information Database accessible at http://www.drc.state.oh.us).

"Ohio Judge Overturns Clemency Granted to Death-Row Prisoners." *New York Times,* February 16, 1991.

"Ohio Woman Gets Death Sentence." *Cleveland Plain Dealer,* June 22, 2003.

"Ohio Woman Put to Death in '54." *Mansfield (Ohio) News Journal,* February 4, 1998.

O'Neil, Melinda E. "The Gender Gap Arguments: Exploring the Disparity of Sentencing Women to Death." *New England Journal of Criminal and Civil Confinement* 25 (Winter 1999): 213–44.

"Only Female Death Row Inmate Describes Poor Conditions." *Lima (Ohio) News,* November 2, 2003.

O'Shea, Kathleen A. *Women and the Death Penalty in the United States, 1900–1998.* Westport, Conn.: Praeger, 1999.

"Ottawa Hills Slaying Suspects Arraigned on Murder Charges." *Toledo Blade,* November 29, 1975.

"'Overwhelming' Doubt that Smith Shot Vinnedge Alleged in Closing Defense Arguments." *Toledo Blade,* September 9, 1977.

Parker, Alex M. "Diar Convicted: Jury Delivers Verdict in Less Than Four Hours." *Lorain (Ohio) Morning Journal,* October 18, 2005.

———. "Diar Gets Death." *Lorain (Ohio) Morning Journal,* November 3, 2005.

"Philip Hahn Submits to Interview on Courtship, Marriage Details." *Cincinnati Enquirer,* August 14, 1937.

"Poison Death Details Bared." *Cincinnati Enquirer,* December 20, 1938.

"Poison Murder Trial to Begin Dec. 8." *Batavia (Ohio) Clermont Sun,* November 20, 1952.

"Police Grill 'Nurse Friend' of Mystery Death Victims." *Cincinnati Enquirer,* August 12, 1937.

"Prosecution Files Brief in Dean Case." *Batavia (Ohio) Clermont Courier,* April 9, 1953.

"Prosecution to Begin Presenting Case in the Vinnedge Murder Trial." *Toledo Blade,* August 31, 1977.

Puente, Mark. "After Burying Son, Mom Sang and Danced at Bar." *Cleveland Plain Dealer,* October 14, 2005.

———. "Burn Victim Faces Trial in Son's Fiery Death." *Cleveland Plain Dealer,* September 26, 2005.

———. "Jury Deliberates Diar's Sentence." *Cleveland Plain Dealer,* November 2, 2005.

———. "Mom Convicted in 4-Year-Old's Home Fire Death." *Cleveland Plain Dealer,* October 18, 2005.

———. "Mom on Trial in Slaying of Son, 4." *Cleveland Plain Dealer,* October 4, 2005.

———. "Mother Sobs before Getting Death Sentence." *Cleveland Plain Dealer,* November 3, 2005.

Ramsey, Nancy. "Portraits of a Social Outcast Turned Serial Killer." *New York Times,* December 30, 2003.

Rapaport, Elizabeth. "Capital Murder and the Domestic Discount: A Study of Capital Domestic Murder in the Post-Furman Era." *Southern Methodist University Law Review* 49 (July–August 1996): 1507–48.

———. "The Death Penalty and Gender Discrimination." *Law and Society Review* 25, no. 2 (1991): 367–83.

———. "Equality of the Damned: The Execution of Women on the Cusp of the 21st Century." *Ohio Northern Law Review* 26, no. 3 (2000): 581–600.

———. "Some Questions about Gender and the Death Penalty." *Golden Gate University Law Review* 20 (Fall 1990): 501–65.

———. "Staying Alive: Executive Clemency, Equal Protection, and the Politics of Gender in Women's Capital Cases." *Buffalo Criminal Law Review* 4, no. 2 (2001): 967–1007.

"Read Anna Marie Hahn's Sensational Confession in Monday, Tuesday Enquirer." *Cincinnati Enquirer,* December 18, 1938.

"Rival Choked and Drowned, Woman Held for Grand Jury." *Cincinnati Enquirer,* September 8, 1952.

Rosen, Richard A. "Felony Murder and the Eighth Amendment Jurisprudence of Death." *Boston College Law Review* 31 (September 1990): 1103–70.

Rosser, Bo. "Jurors Weigh Death Penalty for Mother Convicted of Killing Her 4-Year-Old Son." Court TV, November 1, 1005.

———. "Ohio Mother Receives Death Sentence for Killing her Toddler." Court TV, November 2, 2005.

Sakal, Mike. "Former Home of Nicole Diar May Be Going on Market." *Lorain (Ohio) Morning Journal,* November 17, 2005.

"Sanity Test Ordered for Mrs. Dovie Dean in Poison Case." *Batavia (Ohio) Clermont Courier,* October 9, 1952.

Sauter, Michael. "Killer Chicks; They Shoot, and Sometimes They Score—On Oscar Night, Look for Actresses in Deadly Roles." *Entertainment Weekly Oscar Guide 2004,* February 6, 2004, 52.

Saxon, Wolfgang. "Nelson Gidding, 84, Screenwriter of Classics Like 'I Want to Live!'" *New York Times,* May 14, 2004.

Schmall, Lorraine. "Forgiving Guin Garcia: Women, the Death Penalty and Commutation." *Wisconsin Women's Law Journal* 11, no. 2 (1996): 283–326.

"Sealed Verdicts Returned in Two of Ottawa Hills Murder Trials." *Toledo Blade*, September 21, 1976.

Segrave, Kerry. *Women Serial and Mass Murderers: A Worldwide Reference, 1580 through 1990*. Jefferson, N.C.: McFarland, 1993.

"Seven Jurors Chosen in Hahn Murder Trial; Death Penalty Hinted." *Cincinnati Enquirer*, October 12, 1937.

Shapiro, Andrea. "Unequal before the Law: Men, Women and the Death Penalty." *American University Journal of Gender, Social Policy and Law* 8, no. 2 (2000): 427–70.

Sherlock, Jim. "The Green Mile to Movie Stardom." *Herald Sun* (Melbourne, Australia), April 7, 2004.

Sinkovich, Peggy. "Capital Murder Jury Is Still Being Seated." *Youngstown (Ohio) Vindicator*, May 4, 2003.

———. "Charge of Gun Theft Is Dismissed." *Youngstown (Ohio) Vindicator*, January 10, 2002.

———. "Defense Asks to Move Murder Trial." *Youngstown (Ohio) Vindicator*, April 12, 2003.

———. "Defense to Recall Killer's Childhood." *Youngstown (Ohio) Vindicator*, November 12, 2002.

———. "Hearing Set on Killer's Penalty." *Youngstown (Ohio) Vindicator*, November 21, 2002.

———. "Howland Woman Awaits Verdict in Murder." *Youngstown (Ohio) Vindicator*, May 31, 2003.

———. "Judge to Mull Death Penalty for Jackson." *Youngstown (Ohio) Vindicator*, November 27, 2002.

———. "Jurors Mull Death Sentence." *Youngstown (Ohio) Vindicator*, November 15, 2002.

———. "Jury Deliberates Murder Case." *Youngstown (Ohio) Vindicator*, November 7, 2002.

———. "Jury Issues Indictment of Premeditated Murder." *Youngstown (Ohio) Vindicator*, December 29, 2001.

———. "Jury Recommends Death in Murder Case." *Youngstown (Ohio) Vindicator*, November 16, 2002.

———. "Jury Recommends Death Sentence." *Youngstown (Ohio) Vindicator*, June 8, 2003.

———. "Lawyers Want Statement to Be Thrown Out." *Youngstown (Ohio) Vindicator*, April 18, 2002.

———. "Letters Reveal Scheme." *Youngstown (Ohio) Vindicator,* January 1, 2002.

———. "Man Is Found Shot Dead in Home." *Youngstown (Ohio) Vindicator,* December 12, 2001.

———. "Murder Trial Gets under Way." *Youngstown (Ohio) Vindicator,* October 24, 2002.

———. "Murder Trial Jurors Chosen." *Youngstown (Ohio) Vindicator,* May 16, 2003.

———. "Police Search Car of Man Found Slain." *Youngstown (Ohio) Vindicator,* December 13, 2001.

———. "Roberts' Lawyers Consider Appeal; The Defendant Thanked the Judge after She Received the Death Penalty." *Youngstown (Ohio) Vindicator,* June 24, 2003.

———. "Roberts Makes Opening." *Youngstown (Ohio) Vindicator,* May 17, 2003.

———. "Trial Begins in Howland Killing." *Youngstown (Ohio) Vindicator,* October 8, 2002.

———. "2 Jailed, Charged in Man's Slaying." *Youngstown (Ohio) Vindicator,* December 21, 2001.

———. "Videotape Won't Be Used in Murder Trial." *Youngstown (Ohio) Vindicator,* July 19, 2002.

"Slayings in Ottawa Hills Believed Committed by at Least 2 Persons." *Toledo Blade,* November 21, 1975.

"Slept before Killing Two Women, Arterberry Says in Recording." *Toledo Blade,* September 16, 1976.

"Smiths are Guilty in Holdup, Killing of Jules Vinnedge." *Toledo Blade,* September 11, 1977.

"Son, His Wife, Second Man Charged with Murdering 2 Women in Ottawa Hills." *Toledo Blade,* November 28, 1975.

"Son Visits Mrs. Anna Hahn as Davey's Aide Prepares Report on Mercy Plea." *Cincinnati Enquirer,* December 6, 1938.

"State Is Ready for What Could Be First Woman on Death Row Since '91." *Lima (Ohio) News,* June 10, 2003.

"State Questions Legal Issues in Pardons." *Cleveland Plain Dealer,* May 14, 1991.

"Stepson Released as Officials Probe Death of Farmer." *Batavia (Ohio) Clermont Courier,* September 11, 1952.

Streib, Victor L. "Academic Research vs. Advocacy Research." *Cleveland State Law Review* 36, no. 2 (1988): 253–59.

———. "American Executions of Female Offenders: An Inventory of Names, Dates, and Other Information." 7th ed. Unpublished research report on file with author, July 1, 2005.

———. "Capital Punishment of Children in Ohio: 'They'd Never Send a Boy of Seventeen to the Chair in Ohio, Would They?'" *Akron Law Review* 18 (Summer 1984): 51–102.

———. "Death Penalty for Battered Women." *Florida State Law Review* 20 (Summer 1992): 163–94.

———. "Death Penalty for Female Offenders." Quarterly Web report. http://www.law.onu.edu/faculty/streib/streib.htm.

———. "Death Penalty for Female Offenders." *University of Cincinnati Law Review* 58, no. 3 (1990): 845–80.

———. *Death Penalty for Juveniles.* Bloomington: Indiana University Press, 1987.

———. "Death Penalty for Lesbians." *National Journal of Sexual Orientation Law* 1, no. 1 (1995): 104–26. http://www.ibiblio.org/gaylaw/issue1/streib.html.

———. *Death Penalty in a Nutshell.* 2d ed. St. Paul, Minn.: Thomson West. 2005.

———. "Executing Women, Children, and the Retarded: Second Class Citizenship in Capital Punishment." In *America's Experiment with Capital Punishment: Reflections on the Past, Present and Future of the Ultimate Penal Sanction,* ed. James R. Acker, Robert M. Bohm, and Charles S. Lanier, 301–23. 2d ed. Durham, N.C.: Carolina Academic, 2003.

———. "Gendering the Death Penalty: Countering Sex Bias in a Masculine Sanctuary." *Ohio State Law Journal* 63, no. 1 (2002): 433–74.

Streib, Victor L., and Lynn Sametz. "Executing Juvenile Females." *Connecticut Law Review* 22 (Fall 1989): 3–59.

Sweets, Ellen. "Women Facing Death Penalty in Increasing Numbers." *Dallas Morning News,* May 9, 1991.

"Taped Arrest Statements Ruled Admissible in Murder Trials." *Toledo Blade,* September 13, 1976.

"3rd Woman Pays with Life in Ohio's Electric Chair." *Cleveland Plain Dealer,* June 12, 1954.

"Three Are Indicted in Slaying of Two at Ottawa Hills; Specifications Included Which Could Mean Use of Death Penalty." *Toledo Blade,* December 4, 1975.

"Three at Scene of Vinnedge Slaying Unable to Identify Smith, Court Told." *Toledo Blade,* September 7, 1977.

"Three Poisonings Cases; Investigator is Named." *Batavia (Ohio) Clermont Sun,* September 4, 1952.

"Three Sentenced to Die in Double Slaying in Ottawa Hills." *Toledo Blade,* November 22, 1976.

"To Die for Murder." *Cincinnati Enquirer,* November 7, 1937.

"To Kill Four, Jury Is Told; Defense Is to Call Expert." *Cincinnati Enquirer,* October 20, 1937.

"Trial Marks Anna Hahn." *Cincinnati Enquirer,* October 23, 1937.

"Two Juries Hear Opening Positions in Ottawa Hills Double Murder." *Toledo Blade,* September 14, 1976.

"Two Women Found Beaten to Death in Ottawa Hills Home." *Toledo Blade,* November 20, 1975.

Umrigar, Thrity. "Living Life on Death Row; In Ohio, Two Women Try to Cope Each Day." *Akron Beacon Journal,* April 3, 1989.

Underwood, Jim. "State Questions Legal Issues in Pardons." *Cleveland Plain Dealer,* May 14, 1991.

Verhovek, Sam Howe. "As Woman's Execution Nears, Texas Squirms." *New York Times,* January 1, 1998.

———. "Dead Women Waiting: Who's Who on Death Row." *New York Times,* February 8, 1998.

———. "Divisive Case of a Killer of Two Ends as Texas Executes Tucker." *New York Times,* February 4, 1998.

———. "Texas, in First Time in 135 Years, Is Set to Execute Woman." *New York Times,* February 3, 1998.

"Vinnedge Only One in Charge on Day He Died, Clerk Testifies." *Toledo Blade,* September 6, 1977.

"Wagner and Palmer Poisoned, Report Defense Expert; Gsellman's Death Story Begun." *Cincinnati Enquirer,* October 26, 1937.

"Wagner's Death Is Described by Physicians and Nurses." *Cincinnati Enquirer,* October 17, 1937.

"Wagner's Physician Testifies in Hahn Case." *Cincinnati Enquirer,* October 16, 1937.

"Wagner's 'Will' Forged by Anna Hahn." *Cincinnati Enquirer,* October 28, 1937.

Walker, Charles. "Angel of Mercy—or Angel of Death." *True Detective,* July 1973, 47.

Wanger, Eugene G. "Capital Punishment in Ohio: A Brief History." *Ohio Lawyer,* November–December 2002, 8, 11, 30.

Wernert, Patricia, to Victor L. Streib, October 11, 1990 (letter on file with author).

"Wernerts Accuse Each Other of Conspiring with Arterberry." *Toledo Blade,* September 17, 1976.

"West End Woman Strangled, Drowned in Sharon Woods." *Cincinnati Enquirer,* September 7, 1952.

"Widow Confesses Poisoning Elderly Mate after Trying to Fasten Crime upon Her Son." *Cincinnati Enquirer,* September 13, 1952.

"Will Conduct Hearing on Mrs. Dean's Sanity Monday." *Batavia (Ohio) Clermont Sun,* November 13, 1952.

"Will Roberts End Up on Death Row?" *Youngstown (Ohio) Vindicator,* June 13, 2003.

Wilson, Patrick. *Murderess: A Study of the Women Executed in Britain Since 1843.* London: Michael Joseph, 1971.

"A Woman Condemned to be Hung in Ohio." *Raleigh Register and North Carolina Gazette,* January 12, 1844.

"Woman Found Poisons in Wagner's Dwelling, Hahn Trial Testimony." *Cincinnati Enquirer,* October 19, 1937.

"Woman Indicted on First Degree Murder Charge." *Batavia (Ohio) Clermont Courier,* September 18, 1952.

"Women Should Take Medicine Like Men, Penologist Declares." *Cincinnati Enquirer,* November 9, 1937.